Swing Wide

KERI CARDINALE

BRIDGE
LOGOS

Newberry, FL 32669

Bridge-Logos
Newberry, FL 32669

Swing Wide:
A Story About Love, Sexual Identity, and How God Redefined It All
by Keri Cardinale

Printed in the United States of America

Library of Congress Catalog Card Number: 2019932106

International Standard Book Number: 978-1-61036-400-3

Edited by Lynn Copeland

Cover design, photo credit by Sarah Bridgeman | sarahbridgemancreative.com

Interior design by Kent Jensen | knail.com

VP 01 06/2019

CONTENTS

FOREWORD

In *Swing Wide*, I have discovered the beautiful rebirth and the breathtaking growth of a human, sinful soul. Keri's story is one that must be told in the world in which we live. Because after all, aren't we all sinners? Your sin might look different than Keri's sin did—but we are all sinners in need of a Savior.

We live at a moment in history when it seems as though there are no absolute truths and when the Word of God is sometimes mocked and often discarded. Men and women are making life-altering decisions based upon feelings rather than upon principle or conviction. Keri Cardinale's story is sure to shed light on false assumptions and dismantle cultural bias.

Swing Wide will be the book that you turn to over and over again as you grapple for a guidebook that will answer the tough questions of sexuality and of restoration in God's unshakable Kingdom.

Let me tell you about my dear friend, Keri Cardinale.

Keri is the "real deal"—she is compassionate, she is full of life, and she has a voice that can fill a stadium. Keri is a leader and now she emphatically knows who she is in Christ and what He has called her to be and to do. Keri is gutsy and has never met a stranger. And, let me just tell you that my life would be boring without her zest and her witty conversations. I am honored to be her mentor and her friend. Keri is truly a daughter of my heart!

Keri is that "one-in-a-million" girl who draws people to her like a magnet. When she first told me her story of being delivered from homosexuality, I wanted to stand up and shout! I immediately prayed that the Lord would use her testimony to set many captives free and to be a voice for truth and righteousness in this generation.

Not only has Keri been set free, but she also teaches us all how to love people who may be different than we are. Keri has gently coached me in my relationships with those I didn't understand and thus has helped me embrace the heart of God toward those whom the church has disenfranchised. Keri's story reminds all of us "that while we were yet sinners, Christ died for us" (Romans 5:8, NASB).

Keri has been my worship leader for nearly five years and how I love worshiping Jesus with her! When I observe her lead hundreds and sometimes thousands of believers into worship, I know that "if the Son makes you free, you will be free indeed" (John 8:36, NASB).

Keri Cardinale is a pure gift to the Body of Christ and to a world in pain. She is the living, breathing demonstration that our God is able to take anything—anything at all—and to turn it into something resplendent and beautiful.

The windows of God's limitless grace have swung wide open and have changed the life of Keri Cardinale. Isn't it wonderful to know that what He has done for her He can also do for you and for those you love? Keri's story is a story of hope, of grace, and of miraculous change.

As you read *Swing Wide*, sometimes you will find her story to be raw and at other times it will be redemptive, but it will always be genuine. I dare you to read this book without a box of tissues! I know that when you close the last page of this powerful testimony, you will know the heart of the chain-breaking God in a more intimate way.

I hope that you will use this book as a tool to connect with people who are grappling with their sexuality or with the truth of the gospel message. I hope that you will read it with your children and grandchildren and talk about it. I hope that you will have honest conversations about the issue of sexuality, about the truth of the Bible, and about the power of our limitless God!

CAROL MCLEOD

PREFACE

From my heart to yours:

I ask for you to put on your grace hat as you enter into reading the story of my life. It's a story about one of the most difficult and sensitive topics discussed in the world and in the church. It's also a story filled with heavy memories and, at times, challenging truth. I'm not a preacher, but I do believe it's my responsibility to be a witness of God's character and give people a loving perspective.

I found a love that I have always longed for. Jesus picked me up, cleaned me off, renewed my mind, and rewired my heart and desires. I am changed because of Him. I don't want anyone to miss out on God's goodness. So that's why I agreed to share my heart, my thoughts and opinions, and what God has taught me over the years to help you understand there is more to someone that just a label.

From my heart to the homosexual:

I love you ... and this book is a zero-judgment zone. But that goes both ways. I pray that you are able to read my story without judging me for the life that I now choose to live. So let's not judge each other, okay? I've been challenged enough by friends and people in the gay community, and I am sure you have as well. I want you to feel comfortable entering into my story as if we were sitting across from each other having a cup of coffee. You may even find some parts of it to be familiar to you. I encourage and challenge you to dive into your memory treasure box to see what's there. God may reveal something very special to you that goes beyond "homosexuality." My prayer is that you allow your story to come alive as well—no matter the outcome.

From my heart to the family member or friend of a homosexual:

I share the details of my life with you so that you can get a glimpse into what a potential "day in the life" of your loved one looks like. This book will not teach you how to change someone. I don't believe any of us are that powerful! I hope to give you a fresh perspective on how to build a strong bridge between you both—one that is built with love, respect, and truth. A bridge has two sides; therefore, it takes two to keep it secure.

Thank you for joining me on this journey.

ACKNOWLEDGMENTS

To my mom and dad, who were, and always will be, my biggest encouragers. Thank you for raising me to be loving, compassionate, strong-willed, and bold. It is because you never left my side that I now have the courage to share my story.

To my siblings, Jodi and Sammy, for always being in the "Cardinale Way" with me.

Jodi, thank you for being the person I've always admired and for making me an aunt to Remy and Lulu. Sammy, my brother, thank you for our hugs every time we see each other. I don't think you realize how special they are to me. Thank you for always seeking peace in life. You will forever be our special slugger.

To the love of my life, my husband, Philip James. Thank you for embracing my femininity. I may be a little tough on the outside, but you acknowledge my sweetness and let me be the girl I've always wanted to be. You are my stable ground and my warm fuzzy blanket at the end of a long day. You melt my heart when you surprise me with flowers and tell me I'm dainty! I love you.

Thank you, Michael Chamberlain, for a lifetime of friendship, laughter, and support . . . you are invaluable to me. You know every part of me starting from our days in Cinderella up until this very moment. This friendship means the world to me, and I don't know what I would do without you. I still have every Blue Mountain card you've ever given me! I love you more than my luggage!

Thank you, Sarah Bridgeman, for your constant friendship. You have been the biggest encourager on my healing journey and nudging me along when I wanted to give up. Thank you for teaching me how to be a better friend. And thank you for always capturing the essence of who I am in your pictures. I see myself in a new light because of you. But above all, thank you for grooming me!

Carol McLeod, thank you for taking me under your wing and pouring into my life. Your biblical knowledge and beautiful heart have guided me into the depths of our Father's words, and I can't thank you enough for that. You are my cheerleader and most prominent prayer warrior. Thank you for believing in my voice and my story. Let me tell you something, sister . . . you are the best!

Thank you, Brett Larson, for taking a chance on me when I was a washed-up communications major. You encouraged me to pick up a pen and write, and you gave me a voice on the airwaves. You and the crew at WDCX Radio have left a massive imprint on my heart. It's time to get out your red pen!

A special thanks to Brittney, Ricky, and Valor Perillo for taking in this stray dog! Your home is your heart, and you allowed me to rest my head there for a while. And Brittney, you are my one-of-a-kind friend. Thank you for always allowing our friendship to be exactly what it is with zero expectation. I will forever miss our deep talks about God on your big comfy couch and our temper tantrums on the kitchen floor.

Thank you, Laura Dudek and Dr. Julie Caton, for being my prophetic sisters. You encouraged me from the beginning to be bold and share my heart with the world. Julie, thanks for allowing me to begin writing my story in your home. Your writing room was where these words started to form. Thank you for being the true daughters of our King!

Thank you to the best musicians in the world: Dave Riffel, Danusia Beatz (my crunchy soul sister), Sandy Internicola, and Joe Green. You bring out the best in me! Thanks for always having my back and helping my heart songs come alive!

To my first boyfriend—you know who you are. Thank you for initiating a new friendship with me after all those years. And thank you for clearing up our baggage because I was tired of telling people you ruined my life and turned me into a lesbian. You have become one of my best friends, and for that, I will forever be grateful.

To all the girls I've loved before—you know who you are. You each are very special to me and I'm praying you find true fulfillment in life and in love.

I would also like to thank Anthony and Chris Hoisington, and Justin Reynolds for helping me turn my story into a song: "Swing Wide."

I would have never known I had a story if it weren't for Pastor Jerry Gillis, Benji Cowart, Alan Dusel, and Pastor Deone Drake. Thank you for asking me to be bold enough to share my story publicly.

To Harold Hardin, my first choir director, thank you for teaching me what true worship is. I will never lose my praise, thanks to you.

Thank you, Suzi Wooldridge and the Bridge Logos family, for having faith in my journey and believing I have a story worth sharing.

Finally, Jesus, my true best friend. Thank You for taking the veil off my eyes and for making Your presence known to me. Thank You for sitting with me in dark places and holding my hand. Thank You for always meeting me in the meadow and for letting me lean on Your shoulder. You are my heart and my joy, and You bring fullness to my life. I love You.

INTRODUCTION

I never wanted this to be my story—a story that involves a word that is beyond controversial in our world. For some it stands for love and for some it stands for hate. It divides families, churches, communities, workforces, and our government. You are bullied if you are "for" it and bullied if you are "against" it. This word causes confusion and forces lines to be drawn in the sand. It compels many to live in secret and feel like they don't belong.

The word is "homosexuality"... and it has been rolling off my tongue for the last twenty-five years. I was talking about it while living in a secret closet or while walking in a gay parade. It came up in tense conversations as I defended my identity and in moments when I was proud to be different and unique. It also came up in my quiet time, when I found myself talking to God in the dark hours of the night questioning who I really was when I felt lost and alone—a God I knew existed but was so distant I wondered if I was just talking to myself.

The word "homosexuality" rolls off my tongue much differently now. Some days I wish I could crumple it up into a tiny little ball of letters, hide it away in the back corner of my closet with my secret stuffed animal collection, and never speak of it again. But that doesn't seem to be the plan—well, God's plan. I often get asked about the life I used to live, how I came out of it, and how I keep myself planted on solid ground. The more my story is discussed, the more people are interested in hearing about it. Sometimes it's for their own understanding on the topic as a whole. Other times it's for people who don't know how to respond to a loved one. For some, they like to challenge me that I am still a homosexual or that maybe I never was.

I wrestled with God for many years over this. I'd ask Him why He couldn't give me a reputation for topics like parenting, joyful living, or how to clean your house in one hour. Instead, I get the reputation for the girl who once was a homosexual. I finally surrendered, and it happened the day my testimony was shared at my home church. At first, I was too scared to come clean in front of the congregation. They knew me as their worship leader, not as an "ex-lesbian." I was afraid of being judged for my past. But once I saw my story come alive on video, I realized that it wasn't just my story, it was His story. It became the story of how one girl went looking for love in all the wrong places, and while she was on her love journey, God never left her side. My story became the story about a heart transformed by the love of Jesus. As I watched the video play on the big screen at church that Sunday morning, I knew my life would never be the same. I received a flood of private emails and text messages from people struggling with same-sex attraction, from moms and dads looking for help on how to deal with their child who was gay, and from churches asking for guidance on how to navigate this issue in their congregation. I knew God was calling me to be a bridge in families, communities, and the church.

My story is a love story, not a gay story. It was in the most crucial encounter of my life—when Jesus revealed Himself to me—that I chose to expose my true self to Him. I chose to swing wide the doors of my heavy heart and allow the Lord to hold it close to His own. His gentle, lovingkindness drew me in. Time froze for a moment. The world drifted away, and I knew I was safe with Him. I knew I was with my Creator. That was the day God took my hand and said, "Keri, I know you inside and out. I know how you were made, bit by bit. It's time we take a journey to restore what's been broken. Let Me show you who you really are."

This journey led me to discover who I truly am, and who I was born to be. It allowed me to trade in the world's definition of love and sexuality for God's ultimate truth.

> But blessed is the man who trusts me, GOD, the woman who sticks with GOD. They're like trees replanted in Eden, putting down roots near the rivers—never a worry through the hottest of summers, never dropping a leaf, serene and calm through droughts, bearing fresh fruit every season. The heart is hopelessly dark and deceitful, a puzzle that no one can figure out. But I, GOD, search the heart and examine the mind. I get to the heart of the human. I get to the root of things. I treat them as they really are, not as they pretend to be." (Jeremiah 17:7–10, MSG)

I believe we all owe it to ourselves to take a closer look at our hearts and see what's going on in there. But only God can take you to the depths of it. We can't go back to painful places without His help and strength. We can't. It's too much to take in. And quite honestly, I don't think we are supposed to relive our past. But I do believe, with the Lord's guidance, we can take a look at it to find some roots.

I once believed I was a homosexual, but then I found out there was more to my story. I decided to do some digging, with the Lord's guidance, to help me uncover the truth. I'm amazed at what He has done with my life, and it's my joy to share these fantastic God moments with you!

I invite you to join me in the pages ahead as I relive my memories and share how life was without Christ, my "homecoming," and how my life is now as I live for Christ alone.

CHAPTER 1

Divorced by God

"For a brief moment I deserted you, but with great compassion, I will gather you. In overflowing anger for a moment, I hid my face from you, but with everlasting love I will have compassion on you," says the Lord, *your Redeemer.* (Isaiah 54:7,8)

I love God. I love God more than anything else in this world. But I didn't always feel this way. According to what God says in Isaiah 54:7,8, neither did He.

Whenever I meet a couple, I always ask how they met. Where did it take place? When was the moment they knew they fell in love? I have a few of those stories from my past where I really believed I was in love. But there is something different about my love for the Lord. We have quite the love story. We met, fell in love, fought, split, and reunited again. It's been a long road. But we survived.

For years, though, we lived separate lives. I chose to give myself to others. I cheated on God with men, women, and the world. To be truthful, His love never seemed good enough. I couldn't feel it. I couldn't hug Him or have a full-blown conversation with Him about my day. We didn't go out to eat at a fancy restaurant. I respected God; but He wasn't my companion.

HOW DID IT HAPPEN?

Some people ask me, "How does this all work? How did you become a lesbian? How did you stop being a lesbian? Were you born gay? Are you really not attracted to women anymore? Maybe you never were a real lesbian; maybe it was just a phase."

I'm not here to discuss science. Why? Because I'm not a scientist. Also, science can't answer what's really at the core of my heart. I'm here to discuss just that: my heart. It's what was lacking that allowed me to seek out love in all the wrong places. All the empty spaces, the areas that gave me that temporary fix to what I really desired . . . what I was wired to desire when I was born.

My purpose is to share with you my love story with the Creator of love. I find this world is so quick to jump to the "facts" of life. It's rare that someone actually wants to uncover deep-rooted truths. I didn't want to accept the truth for a very long time. My theme was, "I am who I am, and nobody is going to change me."

The homosexual way of life is more normalized than ever. Many choose to accept it "as is" and move on with their day. But what if there was more to the story? What if "being gay" isn't the issue? What if the issue is deeper and homosexuality is the product? You can choose to accept the homosexual life "as is." But what if you chose to go a little deeper? What if there was a root to homosexuality? Is it possible that it's the product of a deep root of pain buried in the depths of someone's soul?

We often relate our lives to a garden filled with good seeds, bad seeds, and weeds that can take over and destroy all your hard work. Some describe a weed as a plant out of place or a plant growing where it is not wanted. Or weeds are plants that are competitive, persistent, and not intentionally sown. No matter what definition is used, weeds are plants whose undesirable qualities outweigh their good points.

In this day and age, the majority of people don't like to be challenged. But I decided to test myself and allow God to take me on a journey of "uncovering," as uncomfortable as it was going to be, to see what kinds of weeds I had growing in my garden.

We are all searching for that deep sense of love, a love that surpasses all understanding, slaps fear in the face, and is an unconditional blanket that we can cuddle under on the couch. It's the place that feels the most at home, where no matter what happens in life, there is never a question that love is present. It won't leave you or cheat on you. It won't question or confuse you—just accept you. It's the love I always desired as a young girl and the love I searched for high and low, for many years. I got so desperate for it that I fell for many meaningful counterfeits. I say meaningful because I don't want to disregard the love that I encountered in my life.

A LOVE LIKE COFFEE

I like coffee—a lot! I'm willing to drink it as instant, from a gas station, or from a Keurig machine. But there is something different and whole when you drink a cup of coffee from a bean that was freshly roasted. It's real and organic, bursting with flavor! I'd like to meet you wherever you are at, so fill in the blank. If you like wine, then think of the most aged bottle versus wine from a box. If you like chocolate, it's the piece you get in a 99 cent advent calendar versus the piece you bought from Belgium. There is a difference, and your palate knows it.

One day I woke up and really needed a "fix," so instead of waiting for the coffee bean to roast, or the wine to age, or the chocolate to be delivered, I went for the generic. I got my fix, but I wasn't fulfilled. I knew there was something better out there but I was too impatient, so I got comfortable with the generic and just stuck with it. The real thing seemed a bit distant, too "expensive." I couldn't have it all the time. But have you ever noticed how unhealthy the generic is?

Let's talk about that coffee bean for a minute. Instant coffee was created for our convenience, right? We don't even have to wait for the coffee to brew. It's ready once the hot water hits the grounds. Okay, so you crave a good cup of coffee. You can't wait for the good stuff, though, so you settle for the instant. The first sip isn't so good. It's a bit of an acquired taste. But, for the sake of time and caffeine, you take the next sip. Why? Because you want the warmth, the energy from caffeine, and to hold that cup of coffee in your hands. You finish the cup and think, well, it wasn't the greatest cup of coffee, but it served its purpose. You find yourself saying, "I'd much rather have that dark roast cup. I'll get it next time for sure." The next day rolls around, and you don't feel like leaving the house, or you have no time to stop for the good stuff on your way to work, so you go for the instant coffee in your kitchen cabinet. You settle for convenience.

Months later, you find yourself in the routine of drinking instant coffee every morning; the taste is now a familiar one, and you start to enjoy it. You can't even recall the moment you first drank it. But if you did think back, what would you remember? Would you remember that you didn't really like the flavor but you drank it anyway, for the sake of convenience? You learned to love the taste even though if you had the option in front of you, you would, without question, reach for the dark roast. The dark roast cup of coffee almost becomes a distant desire, unattainable. Almost as if you don't deserve it. It's too special. Maybe drink it on special occasions, like a birthday or at a holiday party. Are you following me on this? Are you getting what I'm "pouring out" here?

Okay, now that I have you in my brain a little bit, maybe I'll be able to help you understand how I removed coffee from this story and replaced it with love. That's my story. It's how I desired a deep love that only God could give me and how He became unattainable because I kept choosing the generic version. For me, I've experienced both kinds of love: the real kind and the generic. I now know the difference. But there was a time in my life when I couldn't "taste" the difference.

This is how my desires got shifted and how my wires got crossed.

I'd like to share with you the details of my personal story. It's not the greatest story, but it's connected to the greatest story ever told—the story of Jesus. All my life I searched for this great love. The love that's greater than my dream lover after reading a glittery fairytale. Deeper than the flutter in my stomach when I want to be held, or my first kiss that I never wanted to end. It's more contagious than the melody of a song I can't get out of my head. It's sweeter than the face of a newborn child. It's the kind of love that would be more painful to lose than I can describe. The loss would cause sheer panic, and searching for it would be agony. If you have ever experienced the death of a loved one, then you understand the emptiness of knowing you'll never speak to that person again.

Agony is a strong word. Have you ever experienced it? Let me take you back some years to where it all began for me. Together, we can unravel the tangled cords.

CHAPTER 2

Daydreaming

I was an incredible daydreamer when I was a child. I used to set up my desk lamp as a spotlight against my wall and turn the other lights off. Then it came: the powerful vocal stylings of Whitney Houston blaring out of my cassette tape player. And there I was—well, my shadow—in the spotlight on the wall singing and dancing away with my fake microphone made out of a hairbrush and foil. I would sing as loud as I could! Not just because I thought I could sing, but because it actually felt good to sing out! It wasn't that I liked the sound of my voice, but I just loved the way it sounded with Whitney's voice. My dreams would shatter when my room would shake from my mother whacking her broom on the ceiling from the kitchen below: *"Turn that down or else I'm calling your father!"* One of my mom's famous lines!

As embarrassing as it is now, I would make music videos in my room. Oh, yes, I would set up my dad's VHS recorder and sit at my vanity desk. I'd tune up a sappy pop love song in the background, like New Kids on the Block or Debbie Gibson, and I would sing along as if I were singing about my long lost love. I think we all have those moments as kids, pretending to be in love. Or maybe I'm the only fool to admit it! These music videos I made were about a breakup, though. Not that I had ever experienced one up to this point in my life, but I did know how to cue the fake tears—I had a masterpiece music video!

After I finished receiving my Academy Award for best performance in a bedroom music video, I would stare out of my bedroom window and look up at the sky. *Is there someone out there? Something more than what I knew to be in front of me?* I grew up Catholic, so I knew God existed, but I didn't know to what extent. *God, are You there?...God, can we talk?...God, who are You?...I want to know more of You. Do You have this great love that I dream about?*

I learned at a very young age that I desired love. A love so deep that if it went away, I already knew it would break my heart. As if I was designed to desire and experience something so intense and beautiful that if I lost it, I would be in agony forever. Little did I know at the time that God was revealing to me the love of Jesus.

When I was eight years old, my family moved from Buffalo to New Jersey for my dad's job. I went from attending a private Catholic school to a public school. My sister adjusted pretty well; she found her own way and her own friends. Not me. I was always known to be very happy and jolly, always smiling in Buffalo. But New Jersey had a different effect on me because I couldn't make any friends. I would hang out on the playground by myself during recess while the other kids played kickball, and I always felt out of place. We all have odd memories—like when I would stand in the playground and spin my heels in the dirt. I can still smell the soil. It's a smell that always reminds me of New Jersey. Just spinning in circles by myself, in my own little world. Not by choice, though. I wasn't invited into anyone else's world. My mom tells me I was bullied, but to this day I don't remember it at all. Maybe I blocked it out. It's still a mystery to me. But my mom would come to sit with me at lunch so I didn't have to be by myself.

I struggled with learning in school. I couldn't focus long enough to pay attention, and I didn't enjoy learning new things. I couldn't care less about history or science. Nothing fascinated me ... except for pop music and love songs. One day in math class we had a big test. Our teacher explained that once we finished the test we each had to draw a portrait of ourselves on construction paper, hand it in, then stand in a single-file line and wait for the lunch bell to ring. I felt the pressure because I was the last one to finish the math test and all the students were mocking me for being stupid. Out of complete embarrassment I decided to purposely fail the test. I still had to finish part two of the assignment and draw a portrait of myself. Still holding up the line I knew it had to be quick so I took a yellow crayon, drew a circle, dot ... dot ... dot for my eyes and nose, a quick semi-circle for my smile, and a bunch of swirls around my head to create my horrible perm! Little did I know, when we came back from lunch all of our portraits were hanging around the room in frames. Mine stood out against all the pretty boys and girls with soft colors and cute faces. It was yellow scribble lines with yellow permed hair for all the classroom to see every day until the last day of school. This just gave my classmates another reason to make fun of me—every day.

Second grade has always left an impression on my heart. It was where I experienced rejection. It's when I became good friends with Mrs. Sweets and Mr. Snacks. Food became my source of affection. It certainly felt better eating a Hostess CupCake than exploring the pain of being alone. We ended up moving back to Buffalo after a year, thank the Lord. But I think New Jersey planted a few bad seeds in me. I returned to my Catholic school with a few chips on my shoulder. Not the salt and vinegar ones either, but the chips that forced me to put up walls. I had a hard time trusting if someone wanted to be my friend. Were they fake? Why were they talking to me? Nobody would speak to me in New Jersey, so why would they speak to me now? I figured I'd be nice and pretend to believe them.

Fourth grade seemed to be the age where the boys would torment the girls. I was at the top of the target list with my chubby face. Looking back, I think I was always the chubby girl. I sometimes walk into a room now as an adult and wonder the same thing... will I always be the heaviest girl in the room? Interesting how we are molded at a very young age.

I had a lot of dreams as a child. I wanted to be unique and to be seen. I wanted to be known and loved. This was a theme that followed me throughout my life, never fully being satisfied, always searching for love and acceptance.

This probably explains why I sought out so much attention as a child and caused some unnecessary competition between my sister and me. We are sixteen months apart, and I wanted everything she had! The heart behind this selfishness was that if someone made her feel special, I wanted to feel special too. I didn't understand that I would have my turn when the time was right. I desired the attention and love so much that I stole her moments. One year for her birthday she received a Hello Kitty toy, and I cried so much my parents went and bought me one too. I know, I was a total brat! There was a time when my family moved into a new home. Since my sister was older, she had the first choice of which bedroom she wanted. She chose the bigger room. I cried and whined so hard that my parents eventually gave me the bigger room. But I was too scared to sleep in the room by myself, so I dragged my mattress into her (smaller) room every night to sleep! I became the annoying little sister, and she became the sister I felt safe with. The more I wanted to be a part of everything she did, the more she pushed me away.

My sister and I were very different growing up, except for a few things, like our mutual appreciation for funny movies, music, and being silly. Another thing we had in common was our fists. We fought day and night, and we fought hard. My poor mother! She dealt with it the most while my dad was at work. They did everything they could to keep the competition between sisters to a minimum, but we still battled everything out. One Christmas, my mom left all the price tags on our gifts by accident. We calculated everything to make sure neither of us got more than the other, but were equal to the penny. My mom was very gifted in gift-giving!

I don't know why we fought so much. Some may say because we were so close in age. But after years of us racking our brains about it, I think we both have come to the conclusion that we each thought the other was the favorite of the family—the golden child. Jealousy played a massive role in it. I was jealous of how smart she was and how much attention she got for being "cool." Fashion and style came naturally to her. My sister always had a dream to be a businesswoman. Her vision was always clear, and she made it happen. I am beyond happy for her now, but I envied that growing up. I wish that life made sense to me as much as it did for her. Instead, I became the lost child, roaming from one empty adventure to the next. I had ideas of what I wanted to be when I grew up, but nothing was ever evident.

I annoyed my sister like little sisters do, and she tortured me with horrible names like older sisters do. My annoyance toward her was based on a desire for her attention. All I wanted was to have my successful big sister celebrate me and say, "You're awesome, Keri."

I wish we spent more time together, but it didn't work that way. My dad bought us tickets to see Marky Mark and the Funky Bunch, but after we got into a brawl he ripped them up and grounded us! My parents were all about rules and discipline but when push came to shove, neither liked to punish us. So my dad taped the tickets back together and sent us to the concert. To this day we disagree on how that fight went down. She says I sat on her and crushed her ribcage. I say, maybe so, but it was out of defense for her kicking me. Either way, we got to see our heartthrob, Marky Mark!

One night my parents went out for the evening leaving us home alone. Big mistake. I was singing "Part of Your World" from *The Little Mermaid*. Jodi started screaming for me to shut up. Of course, I just sang louder. She threw my brush down the stairs, so I sang louder. She threw my mirror down and shattered it . . . I sang louder. She ran down the stairs and threw the big dog gate at me! I ran into the other room and grabbed an enormous painting off the wall and threw it at her! I am laughing now, but it wasn't funny then! We cornered each other in the kitchen and started fist fighting. There may have been a knife involved, but I can't say for sure. We then heard the garage door open and panicked! We hurried to clean everything up just in time for our parents to walk in as we went our separate ways. If there was one thing we could have said to each other, it would have been, "Until next time."

We had some good fights. Showstoppers.

During our college years, our family took a first-class trip to France with another family. My sister and I slept in the bell tower of Christian Dior's chateau. Yes, the fashion designer's chateau. We were so fancy. One night they sent us out to hit the town, compliments of my dad's business partner. Well, we lived it up at this hot dance club in Nice, France. We should have been on our best behavior because Princess Stephanie of Monaco was there, but that didn't stop us from drinking champagne and dancing on tables. We had a blast. Somehow the mood turned for the worst, and we ended up fist fighting in the back of the limo-van on our way back to the chateau. As we were punching and screaming profanities, the poor driver didn't know what to do! We snuck into the chateau, all beat up, hoping our parents wouldn't see blood. How we slept in the same room that night, I'll never know. But we woke up, looked at our bruises and laughed it off. Two college girls, still fighting like we were ten years old.

Sibling rivalry. I wonder if it's all because we just wanted love and acceptance from each other. I know that's what I wanted. Jodi probably just wanted to be left alone. But I think she wanted to be recognized for what she brought to the table. I may have overshadowed her with my dramatics, so I don't blame her for resenting me. But just like how I shut down in New Jersey, I started to shut down from my sister. I didn't trust her anymore. I was hurt by the things she said, the names she called me. When she graduated from high school, she left a card on my bed. It was an apology. She wrote:

I'm sorry for what I've said and I would like for us not just to be sisters but be friends.

On the outside, I accepted this. On the inside, I didn't trust it.

My sister was the first person in my family who I "came out" to when I was in my twenties. She was very accepting of it, but deep down I knew she could read right through it. I think she saw that I was living a lie but never challenged me on it. She let me figure things out on my own and was always there for me. Even though I told her the truth about my love life, I still felt like I was hiding. That's how I felt about everyone I came out to. Like I was a fraud. I could never put my finger on why I felt like an outcast.

We had a rough relationship for a very long time. It wasn't until Jodi got pregnant with my niece and nephew that my heart shifted. The moment the twins were born, my pain and hurt just disappeared. I saw her in a new light. She was a mom. She accomplished everything she set out to do, and I was so proud of her. I didn't want to compete with her anymore; I just wanted to be happy for her. We live entirely different lives, but we respect each other now. When we visit her and her family, my mom wants time alone with the kids, and Jodi and I get to go for a walk and grab lunch. The talks we have mean the world to me. I don't operate as if I need it so badly, it's more that I just want to enjoy her company and hear what's on her heart. Babies can knock down the thickest wall. My niece and nephew certainly knocked down my wall with my sister the day they were born.

The shift in my relationship with my sister couldn't have happened without Jesus. He changed me. He turned my heart and my desires. He changed my mindset and filled me with His love. Because of that, I could respond in a healthy way to my sister. We may have lost years of building a good relationship, but what matters now is that we are in each other's lives. No jealousy or envy. No competition or resentment. Just sisterly love.

"I will restore to you the years that the swarming locust has eaten."
(Joel 2:25)

God restores relationships. For this promise, I am grateful.

We all desire things when we are younger. We may not understand it at the time, but through life circumstances our wires get crossed, disconnected, and burned out. I wish I knew then what I know now. I wonder if my relationships would have been different. In life, we are continually searching for true love. But as we search for it, we get side-swiped, distracted, and tripped up. We get pulled in so many directions that the further we walk down a specific path, the more it becomes our identity. At a very young age I was searching for some type of identity. I tried attaching to my sister's identity. I decided to create an identity behind my dramatic personality. But none of it worked. I got lost along the way. The goal is to search for love in the right place, but it's not an easy task. Once I found love in Jesus, my world shifted. Suddenly I could start to make sense of things as if He had given me a superpower to see the truth in everything.

CHAPTER 3

For the Love of Food

There it was, written on my brown-paper-bag-covered book in black pen: FAT PIG. I can still feel the sting now when I think about it. I won't mention his name because he just added me as a friend on Facebook, but I remember that moment clear as day. Sixth grade. English class. Of course, I have forgiven and let it go, but the memory is still there. It was one of those moments in life that sucker punches you in the gut. It doesn't scar you, but you remember what it felt like. This marks the beginning of my career as a yo-yo dieter.

I can only imagine how my mother felt as she watched these kinds of things happen to me. As a mother, how do you help your child? How do you protect your child from being bullied and emotionally hurt, and at the same time stop them from emotionally eating without hurting their feelings? I can only guess she struggled to find the best way to help me. So what's worse, letting your daughter eat until she's five hundred pounds or sign her up for Weight Watchers? My mom made the best choices she could, for which I am thankful. Either way, I was going to have a weight problem my whole life. Dieting was the start of a lifelong battle that I eventually had to surrender to God. I'm glad I learned at a young age to never throw in the towel, to keep learning how to eat healthier and make better decisions on what I put in my mouth. My mom taught me how to fight for what I wanted, and that was to change my ways. It's now our "love language" between each other. When I visit, we swap recipes, and she loves teaching me how to make a complete Thanksgiving dinner and a good bone broth!

Being an overweight child was difficult, and it did some damage to my mindset. I always felt like I didn't belong. I felt different, like everyone was examining me and my body. But I couldn't stop eating. I would binge on whatever I could find. My parents always kept healthy food in the house except on the rare occasions when my mom would bring home a big bag of chips as a special treat! I can't take all the binge blame. The Cardinale family loves food! You put a bag of chips out on the counter and one, two, thr . . . —they're gone! We are like scavengers. Food was a way for us to communicate, especially at the dinner table. It was where we shared stories about the day, laughed at funny jokes, and talked about how delicious our dinner tasted. Either my mom would make her breaded pork chops with applesauce, or my dad would make his pot of sauce and spaghetti with a huge loaf of fresh Italian bread. I did not grow up deprived in the food department! We always ate well. In fact, we went out for dinner often at our favorite restaurants: Chinese, Italian, Polish, seafood, and diners. Our favorite spot was The Beacon in Ontario, Canada, just over the border from where I grew up. Once a month they had all-you-can-eat seafood—including full live lobsters! We would compete to see who could eat the most. My dad always won, and I was in second place (of course), then my sister, and my mom in last place. The only thing missing from those great family dinners was my brother, Sam. But he wasn't born until I was thirteen years old.

I'm not one for keeping journals. I buy them, but I don't really write in them. I have about fifteen journals—all empty except for two. One is from my early childhood years before high school. My sister used to steal it and write funny things in it, like, "Dear Diary, I love Jordan Knight so much it hurts!" Yes, Jordan from the New Kids on the Block. I still have this little pink book with a broken lock on it. I keep it because I can't believe how great a role food played in my earlier years. Every single entry is about food— where we went to eat, what we ate, who ate what! It's crazy but serves as a clue for me, to help me overcome my weight issues now. Here are a few brief samples.

December 25, 1989 (12 years old)

Dear Diary,
Today is Christmas. I got a lot of stuff. I got a stereo, camera, New Kids on the Block poster, and a microphone. Today's schedule was open presents, church, Noni Dottie's to eat, Aunt Linda's to eat, and then to Grandma and Grandpa's house to eat. Let's just say that this was a great Christmas!

December 28, 1989

Dear Diary,
Today we went to Chestnut Ridge. It was fun, but tiring. We went inside for hot chocolate. I had a pretzel and two hot chocolates. After that, we went for dinner. Me, Mom, and Dad each had a fish fry, and Jodi had spaghetti.

January 1, 1991 (13 years old)

Today is New Year's day. I woke up at 1:30 p.m. and went downstairs to eat breakfast. Then Grandpa Sam and Aunt Nancy came over for dinner. We had prime rib, salad, potatoes, bread, and wine. It was good. Then we had strawberry shortcake for dessert. We had fun.

January 2, 1991

Today was okay. I went to work with my dad, and we ate lunch at Karen's Restaurant. Then went to Pleasures & Pastimes for thank-you cards for Sam's christening. Then we ate spaghetti for dinner, and me and my mom went to Weight Watchers. It is my first week.

January 3, 1991

Today was my first day back to school. I did well on my diet. I had grapefruit juice and apple cinnamon oatmeal for breakfast. Apple, pop, and tuna fish sandwich for lunch. I had pizza, but I didn't eat it. For dinner, I had noodles and vegetables in the wok.

April 12, 1991

Dear Diary,
Today we spent the day at the hotel pool. We ate lunch and dinner
there. We also kept going to the games room. For dinner we had
shish kabobs. I had the chicken kind instead of the beef. Then we
went for ice cream. Good night. Love, Keri

April 15, 1991

Dear Diary,
Today was my first day back to school from Easter vacation. It
was boring as usual. I took the bus to my dad's office. Then he
drove me to piano. My mom picked me up, and we went to get
weighed in at Weight Watchers. I gained one pound over Easter
vacation. Then I came home and watched a good movie.

All of my pink diary entries were the same. Short and simple, with a few crumbs of food details and nothing more. I knew I felt sad inside, but I never knew how to express myself as a child.

My weight continued to be an issue all through high school and eventually I hit a wall in college. It was there that a new friend saw me sitting by myself on a porch swing. She walked over to see if I was okay and said I looked so sad. I broke down and told her how much I was struggling with my appearance and eating habits. I had gained even more weight in my first semester and reached an all-time high on the scale. That's when she shared her secret to losing the "Freshman 15": binging and purging. She had been bulimic for quite some time and taught me all the tricks of this horrible disorder that eventually took over my life for a season. I started with a bag of Doritos, then graduated to full-blown meals. She loved to binge for fun and would meet me at the snack machine where we loaded up on cookies, candy, chips, and soda. I felt like I was at a bulimia convention, unfortunately, learning the tricks of the trade.

After a few secret meetings like this, I realized it wasn't fun for me. It remained a way for me to lose weight, but I wasn't interested in having purge parties. Eventually, we stopped meeting and continued our battles separately. My friends noticed I lost weight but saw my attitude shift as I became snappy and moody. Bulimia took over my mind, and I had no control of it. I went home that summer, and somehow my dad found out. He confronted me, and I agreed to see a counselor. Thank God I did because she helped me overcome this disorder. I eventually stopped and never turned back. But my weight issue still nagged my emotions and followed me into my sophomore year of college.

October 1996

Dear God,
There is something wrong with me. I am not going to sit here and tell you how strong I am. Or that everything is great. Nothing is. I feel like I am falling apart. Why can't I be thin? Look at me. I am disgusting. I have tried everything. I'm on my last straw. I can't handle it. I can't deal with the comments and looks from other people. I can't even deal with how I view myself. I know I should leave it in Your hands, but I'm afraid to. I keep gaining and gaining, I can't stop. I was strong enough to stop throwing up. Why can't I be strong enough to stop eating? I don't even know

what is healthy and what's not. I can't do it myself anymore. I need
help. I feel so embarrassed and pitiful.

—Keri

Just like my little pink diary, the green journal from high school and college has just enough entries to provide important markers in my life. My weight played a significant role in how I viewed myself and how I believed I was considered by others, especially boys. I never felt I was desirable, so I put up walls. I couldn't be petite and thin like the other girls on campus, so I embraced a larger-than-life version of me. I chose baggy clothes to hide my physique and developed a robust, intimidating exterior.

I grew up playing golf and started when I was twelve years old. My dad took us out to play one day, and I was hooked. It was really my way of spending time with my dad. He would sign me up for tournaments all over the country, and I got to play on some beautiful courses. I made it to college on a partial golf scholarship, so it was something I tried to take very seriously. I loved the game but secretly hated it for one reason: my weight. My insecurities affected me on a daily basis. We belonged to a classy country club in Buffalo that required tucked-in collared shirts—my nightmare! Not only was I overweight, but I also had the belly to prove it. And every time I swung the golf club I put myself in a vulnerable position to be exposed. I couldn't perform well. Golf is physical, but it's also a mental sport. Any distraction could set your game off. The distraction was a constant sore spot. Sadly, I've never been able to shake it off. It eventually caused me to quit playing in college and lose my scholarship.

I may not be a professional golfer on the LPGA tour, but golf taught me one of the greatest lessons I could have ever learned—a lesson about going back to the basics. Let me tell you a little about my golf swing. I had a fantastic coach who taught me the deep mechanics of the swing, yet my swing was completely mechanical. During my lessons, my coach would videotape my swing and we would watch the tape recording, pausing every second to see my hand, hip, and arm placement.

With having such a mechanical swing, and the mindset of a chubby girl afraid to swing because she was self-conscious, my swing would get out of whack. I would hit the ball beautifully on the driving range, but once I got to the first tee in a tournament, I would blow it. Even as a young girl, I never had a problem speaking in public or singing, and I still don't. Not with golf, though. With only a few people standing there watching, the pressure would make me miss the ball, or shank it right into a bush every single time. I tried to play golf again, years later, but struggled with the same issues. "I don't understand, Keri," my dad would say. "You can sing in front of a thousand people but you can't hit the ball off the tee in front of four people." My excuse for quitting the sport was that I was sick of the game. That was a lie. My body image is what stopped me from playing.

But one thing my coach always taught me when I couldn't hit the ball was to go back to the basics. And the fundamentals of my swing were at the beginning. It was simple: swing up, swing down, hit the ball, and finish high. Once I got that I was okay for a while ... until another tournament crept around the corner.

When we get out of whack with our health or anything else in life, we have to go back to the basics. The basics are God's instruction for our lives found in the Bible.

Even decades later I cried out, "God, what's the deal? Why can't You just have a diet plan in the Bible for me? You have everything else! Why is this so difficult?"

In April of 2011, I found myself in a deep depression about my weight, yet again. As I sat on my couch sulking in self-pity, I turned on the TV to see my favorite pastor, Charles Stanley, preaching about Proverbs 3:5,6. I thought, *Yeah, yeah, I already know this, God.* But He nudged me to get up anyway and read it with my own eyes.

> *Trust in the LORD with all your heart, and do not lean on your own understanding. In all your ways acknowledge him, and he will make straight your paths.* (Proverbs 3:5,6)

I recalled a piece of advice from a friend who encouraged me to read the five verses before and five verses after to understand the fullness of Scripture. So, I kept reading:

> *Be not wise in your own eyes; fear the LORD, and turn away from evil. It will be healing to your flesh and refreshment to your bones.* (Proverbs 3:7,8)

What?! So basically, if I trust God from the bottom of my heart and stop trying to figure out everything on my own, and if I listen to His voice and don't assume I know everything, then He will keep me on track? Will He allow my body to glow with health and make me strong?

God spoke very openly to my heart that night. The conversation went something like this.

God: *I am your instruction. Me. Stop trying to figure it out. Rest in Me. Release this to Me, Keri.*

Keri: *But how, God?*

God: *Do you believe I love you? Just the way you are? Can you look at yourself and see how beautiful you are? Do you think you are worth more than your weight? Keri, I see it all. I know your heart. I know the pain of your weight struggles since you were a young girl. I remember when you were carefree without worrying about how you looked. You were my sweet, jolly little child so full of life. And I know the moments that stole your joy. So let's reclaim them. Focus on Me, and I will guide you to health.*

That night I decided to stop hating myself. I accepted myself exactly as I was: 230 pounds. Not a pound more or less. I decided to stop concerning myself with the lies of what people thought of me, and I decided to focus on my relationship with God. I chose to believe that I was special, and I chose to believe God loves me. This truth gave me a boost of God-confidence, and it still does.

But the battle of the bulge has been a long road for me, and it continues to overpower my mind. Certainly not as much since I started to rely on the Lord for strength, but the struggle is real, and it creeps up on me every once in a while. Counseling has been a massive support in helping me break down the years of emotional layers on my body. I'm still learning, and the weight is coming off. But it's no longer my main concern. My main focus is being secure in Him, how He sees me, and how He loves me. There are days when I don't like what I see in the mirror. But then I take practical steps to capture the negative thoughts. I go back to the basic instructions God laid out for me, and I am reminded:

For you formed my inward parts; you knitted me together in my mother's womb. I praise you, for I am fearfully and wonderfully made. Wonderful are your works; my soul knows it very well. My frame was not hidden from you, when I was being made in secret, intricately woven in the depths of the earth. Your eyes saw my unformed substance; in your book were written, every one of them, the days that were formed for me, when as yet there was none of them. (Psalm 139:13–16)

After reading these beautiful God-inspired words, my heart shifts, my mind gets reset, and I am not only ready to fight temptations that come my way, but I am also able to see myself as a beautiful woman—extra pounds and all. Don't get me wrong, I want the extra pounds gone. But I can't start the process until I take a good look at the whole story. I want a healthy relationship with food, and I know God wants the same for me.

CHAPTER 4

Growing Up Catholic

Tradition. It's part of the Cardinale heritage. We breathe it, speak it, and eat it. I could probably go so far as to say that tradition is what has kept us close over the years. It's what disperses arguments and brings us back to a loving place. This goes beyond just my immediate family. It's what helped my dad and his brother talk again, and it's what has kept my mom and her parents close. Religious traditions are just as important in my family because they are a sign of the faith. From one generation to the next, we were all taught to go to church every Sunday and take communion, go to confession, don't eat meat on Fridays during Lent, get the Easter baskets blessed, and love each other unconditionally. If you're looking for a good fish fry in Buffalo, our family knows the hotspots!

I was born in Lackawanna, New York, the home of Father Baker and the Our Lady of Victory Basilica, the place where I experienced reverence for God at a very young age. To give you a picture of this place, it was built as a replica of St. Peter's Church in Rome, Italy. To say it's grand is an understatement. It's powerful. Everything about the Basilica is overwhelming—the ceiling, the statues, the pews, even the silence you experience when you're the only one in there. It's so quiet that it actually hurts your ears a bit. But I love the story behind the building. Father Baker reminded me of Mother Teresa, as they both had a love for the poor. His passion was for the unloved child. He was a simple man with big faith. He built the Basilica with donations that came in from all over the world. Even though my home church was grand in size, I felt the smallness of it. It was home to me. It still is, in a way. It's where I go when I can't think straight. It's a bit like a prayer closet for me. Well, maybe a mansion's walk-in closet! When life gets heavy and I want to spend some quiet time with God in a safe place, I'll go there to sit by myself in a pew and just be silent. Even to this day, I'll go after work when there's only the custodian mopping up the marble floor. And I sit. Fight the noise in my mind. And just relax. How amazing it is to sit in the presence of Almighty God. There aren't words to describe it. I can close my eyes right now and imagine that space in the pew.

A few years back, I went to sit in the Basilica to spend time with God. I remember leaving work and having a strong desire to hear from God. I was the only person in the building, and the silence was very overwhelming. I sat in the pew and told God, *Okay, here I am. Speak to me. I need to hear from You. Just say something, say anything to me.* Looking back, I think I was struggling with faith. I needed some extra proof that He was there. Reminds me of being in a relationship. The other person tells you they love you, but sometimes you just want to be reassured by hearing the words. So I sat and waited. But nothing. My mind kept wandering off, and I had to force myself to sit in silence until I heard something from God. But nothing.

So I decided to walk around. The Basilica is lined with life-sized statues replicating the stations of the cross. As I got to the station where Jesus fell the second time, I stood there for a moment. The longer I stood, the harder I stared. The statues almost came to life. I started to see the movie in my mind and watched this scenario play out. Then reality set in. Jesus suffered. He really suffered. Sometimes as Christians we forget this part. We sing about it, praise and worship about it, and throw big words around describing what Jesus did for us. But that very moment, I connected with His pain. How lonely He felt. How much pain He was in. How uncomfortable it was to carry a heavy, prickly wooden cross on His raw back. I can't even handle doing a set of squats at the gym, let alone carrying a wooden cross up a hill, with everyone screaming around me, yelling that they want me to die, spitting on me, pushing me, and being tortured to keep moving. Jesus kept falling down. Of course He did. Nobody is strong enough to handle that burden. Not even Jesus in His humanity. How did He do it? He probably couldn't hear His Father clearly and felt like God was gone too. He just knew what His mission was. There were some people along the way who loved Jesus enough to help Him up.

As this reality was playing out in my mind, I started weeping right there in front of this piece of art depicting Jesus' life. More like sobbing. And I just cried out, "What can I do for You??" There I was, waiting for God to do something for me, to speak to me out of my own disbelief and lack of faith. God had led me to stand up and walk around and had led me right to the statue of Jesus falling. Through that moment of focusing on Jesus, I heard God. But He didn't have to say one word. The reality of Jesus brought me to my knees. I was humbled. I wanted to serve Him. My moment of desperation turned into a moment of a mission. I walked out of the church that evening with a new sense of worth.

Jesus, I see what You did for me. I see the struggle You went through so that I can have a new life. I'm done complaining. I'm done whining. I'm done acting like I don't have faith. Because I do have faith. I want to be on Your mission team, Jesus. Lead me to where You want me to go. Show me where to serve, show me how to love, prepare my heart for the battles I'll have to face in life, and give me the courage to step out and help someone when they fall the first, second, and third time. Pick me, God! Use me, God! I want to be just as close to Jesus as the person who helped Him up on the road to His death. Thank You, God, for rewiring my thoughts as I sat in that pew. Thank You for being silent, so that I could stand up and walk around to see what's really going on in life besides my own sob stories.

I walked out of my old Catholic church home with a new mission that day.

I found my faith when I was fifteen years old. I had a bunch of questions on a sheet of paper that I brought to my priest. Why do I honor the pope? Why do I pray the rosary? Why do I pray to the Virgin Mary? What is this all about? It doesn't make sense to me. But he wouldn't answer the questions in detail. Instead, he gave me the greatest advice. He told me to visit a service that was held in the basement of the Basilica every Tuesday night. So there

I was, sitting in the basement in a very unfamiliar setting. I was the youngest one in attendance by maybe twenty-five-plus years. There was a little band and they were singing happy songs about God. Nothing like what I was used to singing upstairs from the hymnal led by the intense organist. Everyone was singing along, clapping their hands and holding their arms up in worship. They had smiles on their faces. Some had their eyes closed and were singing with such joy and adoration. I was surrounded by people who were having personal encounters with the Holy Spirit. The priest who led the service was my favorite priest in the church, Father Dimitri—super happy and loved to sing! The service typically lasted around ninety minutes. We sang, we prayed, we shared stories about how God moved through our lives that week. There were moments when I would hear a voice from the back of the room, speaking a language I didn't understand. I remember turning around to see what was happening, and a woman stood with her eyes closed, hands open, and prayed in another language. She looked so peaceful and beautiful. I wondered what she was saying. I wanted to speak that language. It was as if it was a special language between her and God. I sat there admiring what she was experiencing, like a little kid watching a sailor kiss his bride for the first time. My eyes and ears were glued to this woman. Yes, I know, sounds a bit shocking coming from a Catholic church, but the Spirit was in that basement every Tuesday night. I couldn't wait to go back. I started inviting my friends, and we had a whole row of high school kids every week! We studied the Bible and learned about Jesus.

Of course, my favorite part was the potluck dessert table awaiting our presence directly after service. Someone always made this chocolate marshmallow concoction that I couldn't wait to get my hands on! Once I had my sugar fill, then I could engage in conversation with the others.

These Tuesday night services taught me how to pray. I prayed every night in my room, quietly, with the hope of experiencing God. Sometimes I would lie in bed for hours lost in prayer. But I wouldn't say anything. I would just rest in God's presence. It was my favorite place to be.

My parents enrolled my sister and me in private Catholic schools from pre-K to elementary and all the way through high school. Our classes were always small, disciplined, and full of nuns. They were tough but sweet and loving at the same time. I once was chased around the classroom by a nun with a stick! Since she couldn't catch me, she slapped me with a detention slip! I'm grateful I went to private schools. They taught me the importance of one-on-one. Out teachers were attentive and dedicated to the students. I was able to try out all different types of extracurricular activities and became an avid cheerleader. I was proud to be the superstar sixth grader on the varsity team! Cheering allowed me to be loud and expressive. At one point I won the "most spirited cheerleader" and felt like I was good enough to be a part of a team. My cheerleading days ended in eighth grade, but I will always have fond memories of French-braided hair, pom-poms, and Keds. My favorite part of private school was our uniforms. I loved my plaid uniforms even though they stumped my fashion growth. I don't think I figured out my own style until I was thirty! I secretly wish I could still wear my plaid jumper or kilted skirt and call it a day.

High school was a bit different. I attended a private, Catholic, all-girl school. Mount Mercy Academy is an old, beautiful red brick building in the heart of South Buffalo. Back when I was a student we had a reputation for many things, like having down-to-earth and fun-loving students. South Buffalo has a large Irish population so you could guess we also had the reputation of being heavy drinkers. Unfortunately, some people called it the "red brick whore house." Girls came out either pregnant or a lesbian. I tried to graduate without falling into one of those categories, but that didn't happen.

If I had the chance to redo my high school years, I would still choose Mount Mercy. There were no boys to rate our beauty, we could be ourselves, and I think we invented the "hipster" messy bun look without trying to be cute. Girls could be girls. From hairy leg competitions to class clowns, we were free to be silly and learn about what inspired us. We had the typical bullies who tried to rule the hallways but, all in all, we worked together in building friendships, developing our minds, and cheering each other on. It was like one big sorority.

I thrived in high school, but not as a student. I flourished in everything else except my grades. Every quarter I would confiscate my report card from the mail and hide it in my room. My mother, the detective and best snoop of all time, would sniff it out and give it to my dad. It was routine. My dad would call me downstairs, sit in his recliner, and I would sit on the edge of the couch. He would sternly talk about my failing grades, and my lack of doing chores around the house, and tell me I could always do better. I would try to apply myself to my studies, but they weren't interesting enough to keep my attention. It's a horrible excuse to not learn, but that was how my mind works. This happened all the way through college. In fact, I didn't truly apply myself to studies until I went back to school at the age of twenty-nine for massage therapy. My mind finally woke up, and I enjoyed the art of learning.

I did my best to stay out of drama and stick to my bubbly personality to survive all four years of high school. I joined a club called Oratory & Debate, became Student Government President my senior year, and embraced the musical theatre scene. I finally had the guts to audition my sophomore year and got my first role in our high school musical, *Godspell.*

This was the same year I encountered Jesus. In fact, it was the script of *Godspell* that allowed the Bible to come alive for me and I got to be a part of it. *Godspell* was a special time in my life. I was asked to sing two solos in the musical, "Day by Day" and "All Good Gifts." I remember the first time I sang "Day by Day" in front of the cast and crew. Singing about Jesus flipped a switch on in my spirit. My heart was ignited, and I felt something special. Everyone in the room, including myself, was in tears. I knew at that moment I was created to sing for Jesus. I remember hearing the words of Matthew and learning about the teachings of Jesus. As we acted out the gospel in true *Godspell* hippie form, my heart came alive. I can't even begin to express my love for Jesus. It was like falling in love for the very first time. I couldn't wait to go to church every Tuesday night.

These were the beginning days of my own evangelism movement. I would sit in the cafeteria and read to people the incredible stories of Jesus and share my thoughts on what they meant to me. I wanted my friends to experience the awe and wonder I had running through my veins. My good friend at the time, and still a fantastic friend, would sit with me at lunch and eat her cereal as we talked about the Bible. It became my mission to invite everyone and anyone to that little Tuesday night church service in the basement of the Basilica. At one point I brought enough people to fill two long pews! There we were, a bunch of crazy high schoolers, in the midst of fifty- to seventy-year-olds hungry for faith.

Catholicism will always be a part of my faith walk because it's where I first experienced the presence of God. I am no longer a practicing Catholic and choose to label myself a Christian. I'm a Christ follower who believes in the power of the Father, the Son, and the Holy Spirit. I experience each entity on their own, and all three as one. I'm not a fan of anyone who demeans Catholicism either, because I see the beauty in it. It's where I found my faith. But I did have to shift away from the Catholic doctrine because I never learned about how to have a relationship with the Lord. He was always a distance away from me. As a child, I yearned to be close to Him; I just didn't know how to get there. And following rules and regulations, praying to the saints, and indulging in a fish fry during Lent didn't make the connection either. I wanted more.

I will forever be grateful for that little Tuesday night service in the basement of the Basilica. It was the sweetest church I had ever experienced and still is to this day. That group of charismatic Catholics had a love for Jesus that was authentic and real, and I could see just how much Jesus loved them too. It was a beautiful exchange and one that will forever be implanted on my heart. It was this experience that I clung to when I stepped away from my faith and stepped into the scary world.

Unfortunately, the wilderness walk was not very kind to me. The devil grabbed my heels every step of the way. The deeper I operated in the ways of the world, the further away I got from Jesus. He became a distant memory. Every once in a while I would experience spiritual homesickness, which caused me to search for Jesus. I knew deep down He was something special and no matter what came my way, nothing could compare to His love.

From homosexuality, poor relationships, and bar hopping, to Buddhism, the occult, and psychic studies, to becoming a Reiki practitioner, seeking out the spirit in a sweat lodge, and praying Jesus would fly out of a crystal rock if I held it close enough to my heart, I never gave up. I could look at my life and think, *Wow, Keri, you really messed up.* But it's really the story of one girl searching for her soulmate, believing He was out there, and never giving up. Crawling through the swamps in life, dying of thirst in the deserts, surviving the storms, and climbing the mountains...I knew Jesus was out there. I was determined to find Him someday.

In the meantime, I would carry guilt in my heart and live in the made-up belief that God would never forgive me for what I did.

CHAPTER 5

Faith Come and Gone

He left me. God left me. He turned His face from me. He really did. I can remember the moment clear as day. I was sitting in my Tuesday night church service in the basement of the Basilica, the Tuesday after my boyfriend and I slept together.

We met when we were fifteen years old through mutual friends. It was a blind, double date that was typical for teenagers. My friend's mom dropped us off at the mall, and I was so nervous. I kept whining about how I thought he wouldn't like me. My insecurities were coming on strong. Just as we pulled up to the mall, I thought, *What if I don't like him?*

We met the boys near the food court, and sure enough, I wasn't interested. I immediately felt the pressure slide off my shoulders. We walked around the mall for a bit then ended up at Pizza Hut. He was a nice guy, but I could tell neither of us was interested in the other. Until one night on the beach.

He ended up driving me home after a party on the beach a month after we met. We started talking about our faith and how he had been a Christian his whole life. A month later we were dating. We had so much fun together! We laughed at the same weird jokes, loved the same type of music, and had great conversation. Our like for each other turned to love, and we chose to put it to action. We decided to give each other something that belonged only to God: our virginity.

I knew something shifted that night, for both of us. I knew that moment affected our walks with the Lord. I think I can relate to Adam and Eve in the garden. I can't remember details of that night, but I do remember losing more than just my virginity. If I could paint a picture, it would be me and my boyfriend lying next to each other with a little confusion in our minds. There was a thick grayish cloud covering the sky, with a thin fog coming down from the shadows that made it difficult to see what was in front of us. We could hardly see each other, that's how thick the fog was—almost like a natural veil. This misty veil formed in front of us, and we had the strong sense we were on the other side of "something" (not sure what that something was). I think after those few moments of lying there, we got up and resumed our normal conversation.

But I do distinctly remember a moment of separation in the air. I couldn't put my finger on it, but something did shift that night. I can guess it's the same foggy veil Adam and Eve saw the moment they ate the apple. A shift. A cloud. A misty veil. Confusion and an odd sense of separation from "something." The feeling you get when you realize you left your wallet on the subway bench. Immediately you panic, then your thoughts begin to form. You start walking back and follow your footsteps to where you last stopped. You can see the movie in your mind. You sat down, took out your wallet to put your subway card away. You painfully see yourself laying it on the bench when your phone rang. It's the moment of realization. You see it. You see yourself leave your wallet on the bench and walk away. You run back frantically praying it's still there. As you run back, the thought comes to mind, *What if it's gone?* Panic.

That Tuesday in church, I started to see the movie in my mind as I thought back to that night. *What did I do?* I couldn't lift my head up. I physically couldn't lift it up. The tears kept falling. It was the first time in my life I wept. I truly wept. I knew. I just knew I lost something. I couldn't shake it off. I didn't even understand what I was feeling. All I knew was that I couldn't feel God's presence. It was not there for me. The gray cloud went from the sky and transferred into my heart. I became empty and dark.

I loved Jesus. But I gave my heart to my boyfriend along with a part of me that was God's property. In a moment of God's anger toward me, for a brief moment, He deserted me and hid His face from me. I felt it. It was heavy and empty at the same time. I wanted to run to my boyfriend, but something shifted for me there as well. I felt distant from him after what we did. I honestly felt too vulnerable. I knew he was struggling with it also. Ashamed to reach out to God for forgiveness, feeling like I lost my lifeline to Jesus, embarrassed to share these feelings with my boyfriend...I needed comfort so I turned to the one who loved me, my best friend from school.

In the fall of 1995 I made my way to Florida for college. After many failed attempts to make our relationship work, my boyfriend and I broke up and I was ready to take on the college campus life! Truthfully, I was so scared. I've always been a social butterfly, but college intimidated me. I was comfortable coexisting with girls in school, but boys took it to a new level. All of a sudden I felt like people were viewing me with X-ray vision, looking me up and down, and judging every roll on my body. These were the nineties; everyone wore Birkenstocks, cut-off jeans shorts, and brown braided belts. I was filled with jealousy as I watched groups of girls pass by with their short shorts, tank tops, and pretty hair. I felt like there were swarms of territorial posses everywhere and I stood, alone, in the middle of it all.

I was lucky enough to have a single dorm room, so I would lock myself away and drown in my sorrows with Sarah McLachlan's "Surfacing" album on repeat. I missed my life in Buffalo. But I missed Jesus the most, and for some reason, I couldn't find Him. In my four years of college, I think I remember the Florida humidity the most, though I do remember how empty I felt. Minus a few good friends, I don't have many fond memories. I have some pictures that captured "fun" times but what stands out the most was my sadness. Of course, nobody could detect this in me because I was a genius at covering it up. But it was there. And so was emptiness.

Emptiness consumed my life. It was in every cigarette I smoked, drug I took, class I skipped, and test I cheated on. Emptiness was in every lie I told and every person I slept with. My life was one big, depraved lie.

September 28, 1997 (junior year of college)

Dear God,

What can I say? What the heck has happened to me? I once was a girl who was wrapped around my faith's finger. Nothing could harm me. I used to feel my faith overpower me; I am lucky if I can even say the word now. Why? Why has this happened to me? Who has done this to me? What sin did I accept that pushed me so far away from the true love that I once had in my life? The love that saved my life from the darkness. Right now I feel as if I am in the center of a monstrous tornado. Sin swirls around me with such power I can't break through the horrible spirits that drag me to my grave. When did these chains form around my heart where I can't be set free?

In a matter of about five years, I have managed to lose my faith, lose my moral beliefs, change my sexuality, and change my entire outlook on life, where now my outlook is absolutely nothing! I don't think. And if I do try to think, it's of nothing special. Striving for unanswered questions is no longer a fantasy of mine. There are moments when I try to break through to get closer to You, but I always hit a wall.

October 27, 1998 (senior year of college)

Dear God,

Everyone makes me miserable. I lay around all day, and my motivation is gone. I am constantly snapping at the people that are trying to help me. Like my family. I turn my back on them. Why? They care about me so much. They would give me the world, and I take them for granted. They are good people and just want the best for me. I can't expect them to understand me when I refuse to let them in. I push them away. I am scared to let them know the real me. Well, I am not the "real me" right now. That's what I need to find. But how? I am so confused as to who I am supposed to me.

I feel like I have this other person living in me, not physically, but someone who is screaming to be let out, someone who knows the real me.

How can I open up to my family? How can I be me? How do I get God? NO—how do I get back into God's world? I know this is where I will find my happiness.

As I read through my old journal entries, I am overwhelmed with how empty my spirit was at that time. My heart expressions only describe the truth that is found in Romans chapter 1. It's a heavy one, but stay with me.

For the wrath of God is revealed from heaven against all ungodliness and unrighteousness of men, who by their unrighteousness suppress the truth. For what can be known about God is plain to them, because God has shown it to them. For his invisible attributes, namely, his eternal power and divine nature, have been clearly perceived, ever since the creation of the world, in the things that have been made. So they are without excuse. For although they knew God, they did not honor him as God or give thanks to him, but they became futile in their thinking, and their foolish hearts were darkened. Claiming to be wise, they became fools, and exchanged the glory of the immortal God for images resembling mortal man and birds and animals and creeping things.

Therefore God gave them up in the lusts of their hearts to impurity, to the dishonoring of their bodies among themselves, because they exchanged the truth about God for a lie and worshiped and served the creature rather than the Creator, who is blessed forever! Amen.

For this reason God gave them up to dishonorable passions. For their women exchanged natural relations for those that are contrary to nature; and the men likewise gave up natural relations with women and were consumed with passion for one another, men committing shameless acts with men and receiving in themselves the due penalty for their error.

And since they did not see fit to acknowledge God, God gave them up to a debased mind to do what ought not to be done. They were filled with all manner of unrighteousness, evil, covetousness, malice. They are full of envy, murder, strife, deceit, maliciousness. They are gossips, slanderers, haters of God, insolent, haughty, boastful, inventors of evil, disobedient to parents, foolish, faithless, heartless, ruthless. (Romans 1:18–31)

I know it sounds a bit dramatic, but it's the truth. Maybe I didn't murder anyone nor was I a God-hater, but I did wreck hearts around me and I was extremely disobedient to my parents. I was filthy inside and out and sexually confused. I didn't treat God the way He deserved to be treated. He had every right to be angry and turn away from me. And I did pay for it. I was *emptied of God and love, godless and loveless.*

Depression stayed close to my heart for years as I walked this earth without the Lord by my side. I found myself wandering in the wilderness. Just like the Israelites who wandered for forty years, I too struggled with unbelief and rebellion. I refused to give up my own understanding of life, and I chose to sulk in my misery. There was a way out, but I was too disheartened even to consider it. So I stayed in my pit of despair.

The only thing that brought me some sort of pleasure was music. After college, I moved to Nashville to pursue a music career. Music was my source of comfort, but at the same time, it allowed me to stay in my despair. My dad had a friend who produced music and offered to help me create a demo, so I jumped at the opportunity, only to find myself even more depressed in Nashville. I hadn't the slightest clue what I was doing in the music scene. Nashville is a place that requires you to pay dues. That means time invested in the community, networking, taking as many hole-in-the-wall gigs as you can get, and working your tail off to make ends meet.

My style of music had no business in Nashville. There I was, smack dab in the middle of country music and gospel, with my electronic dance music. The only places I fitted in were the gay bars. I attempted to pick up late-night gigs, but they were few and far between. My favorite one was in the middle of the country. Our stage was a car trailer on the back of a pickup truck, and the audience sat on haystacks. I didn't know what I was in for so I went prepared in my club costume, an all-white outfit with knee-high electric blue boots! I even brought my gay dancer friend from the nightclub who wore goggles as an accessory. No, we did not fit in! I even auditioned to be a karaoke host! The only song I knew in the book was "Genie in a Bottle" by Christina Aguilera. Needless to say, I didn't take the job. Instead, I landed a position as a bank teller. My best friend, Michael, from Buffalo moved to Nashville a few months after I got there, and we immediately settled into the club scene.

Just as much as we were both seeking a place to belong and a group of people to be in community with, we were also searching for a church. I still had remnants of my faith lingering and was hoping to include Jesus back into my life somehow. But the nightclubs won the weekend battle and kicked the early Sunday morning alarm clock across the bedroom.

Michael finally had enough of our Nashville ventures, and he moved back to Buffalo. At the same time, I rekindled a relationship with a friend from college who decided to move down south to live with me.

She was more extroverted than I was and made friends easily. I still struggled with trusting people, but I followed her lead and we became part of the Nashville gay scene. Sex, drugs, drag queens, and underground clubs were life as we knew it, and my hopes and dreams of becoming an artist quickly faded.

I decided to trade in my cowboy boots for sequins and move across the country to Los Angeles. Surely there was a music scene for me out there. So we packed up our lives and waved goodbye to Nashville. LA was a fresh breath of air, at first. There was sunshine, smoothies, and the smell of suntan lotion—and people smiled! It was a cultural melting pot. But they don't call it the city of broken dreams for nothing. Everyone is trying to catch a break and find themselves at the same time, all while trying to hold down a job, pay an obscene amount of money for rent, and put food in their mouths.

We landed an apartment in the heart of Hollywood. It wasn't ideal for two suburban girls from New York, but we made it our own. We had little or no money, so we found all of our furniture on garbage night. We carried an L-shaped couch three blocks! Hey, it was free. We slept on a blowup mattress that had a hole in it, and our dinners were dollar store creations: pasta, butter, and garlic powder. I called it Pasta Poor-ay.

I tried to connect to the music scene but that was another bust, just like Nashville, and the only stage I was getting was at gay karaoke. An all too familiar pattern began to form. I would go, give it my all, and then decide at a certain point that I had failed—and then stop again. It never felt like our lives were getting better. After a dead body was found in our apartment building, along with rats in the walls, we decided to sell everything we owned, pack up the car with the basics and our sweet rescue dog, and head back to Western New York.

Dreams faded, faith was lost, and all hope was gone. Life became gray. I can identify with Paul:

> *When neither sun nor stars appeared for many days, and no small tempest lay on us, all hope of our being saved was at last abandoned.* (Acts 27:20)

Whatever faith I had in God was coming to an end. Whatever communication I had left with God was going to silence. Doubt filled my heart. I eventually grew dark inside, and I became numb to everything around me. I finally gave up my dream to sing and put my vocal cords under lock and key. I accepted my despair, lowered the shade, and crawled under my blankets. I was done with everything. My faith was officially gone.

CHAPTER 6

Intimate Skeletons

We all have memories that we prefer to leave in the box, or brief periods in our lives that we shove to the end of memory lane. I have a few doozies that typically revolve around stupid dating decisions I've made. Like the British bloke from England that I met on DatingBritishguys.com. Or when I dated a random redneck ex-con wearing Wrangler jeans and missing teeth. I call it "theme dating." This time around, the theme was a rodeo cowboy. He was nice...but wow was I off. It just didn't work. I'm a city girl. I prefer a high-rise condo over a country home any day. I feel safer on a busy street than I do walking down a country road. I'm not a gardener and don't plant flowers. My mom jokingly asks my sister and I what happened to her daughters because she loves gardening, planting herbs, and fresh flowers. How did she bear two girls who couldn't care less? Don't get me wrong, I love fresh flowers and herbs and garden veggies. I just don't want to be the farmer—I'd rather be the hustler selling the crops!

Okay, back to those memories. Or should I call some of them intimate skeletons collecting dust in my closet? Skeletons that go deeper than the redneck ex-con. Memories that I don't like to touch. I know they are there, but there is a lot attached to them. Sometimes I pull one out just for the sake of shock-value entertainment for my friends. It's safer for me to say it, own it, and laugh it off. Like in my New Age occult days when I dabbled in urine therapy. Oh, yes—drinking my urine for medicinal purposes. It's a real thing out there. Of course, those were my "searching" days. Oh, the things I would do to find Jesus again, trying everything under the sun. But that's a story for another time.

There are more profound, more intimate memories that I'm, quite honestly, scared to share. It's not that I'm afraid of judgment, but more that it makes me sad. I have flashback moments. Scenes play in my head, and I have to shake them off and remember who I am now. But I know the only way for you to get a glimpse of my world is for me to go back to some of those places.

As for the people I describe in the stories you are about to read, they will remain anonymous for the sake of their privacy. I would also like to add that each and every person I was in a relationship with meant the world to me. They were not only my girlfriends, but they were also my best friends at different seasons of my life.

I was twelve years old the first time I laid my eyes on a *Playboy* magazine. Without throwing anyone under the bus, I'll just say I found them stashed in the bathroom of a home I visited every once in a while. This isn't something I like to admit or even talk about, but I know it's part of the process. These are critical moments in my life that help me map out how and when my wires got crossed.

I can remember the first day I saw the cover of the magazine. I was curious, so I picked it up. As I sifted through the pages I saw things that I've never been a witness to before. Body parts that I had as a girl but didn't realize made me feel a certain way until I had visual contact. I saw pictures of men with women, men with men, and women with women. I can't say what turned me on specifically, but it was the overall stimulation that I experienced when looking at something sexual. I have this overwhelming sense of sadness as I write these words because these are the moments in a child's life that start to shape their minds and hearts. I was fascinated by what I saw. I wanted to see more. They must have thought I was extremely constipated with the amount of time I spent in the bathroom! I wanted to know what the men and women in those *Playboy* magazines were feeling. Were they feeling what I was feeling? I want to try those things. My innocent heart. There I was, twelve years old, staring at the filth and being so mesmerized by what I was feeling inside. I wanted more. Where could I find it?

THE FIRST ENCOUNTER

There was a girl I knew when I was in middle school. We used to play Barbie dolls all night. In fact, we did a lot together. We rode our bikes, had street picnics, swam in our pool, played Nintendo, and watched movies all night, not to mention raiding their stocked pantry of chips and dip. Every weekend we would play board games, listen to the top 10 at 10 and record our favorite songs onto cassette tapes. My memory is a bit faint on this one, but I do remember she was the first girl I ever kissed. I don't know how we ended up on her bed, but somehow we found our hiding spot under the covers. I don't believe we went any further than kissing—I hope that's the case. But this is where it began for me.

Maybe it was lack of attention or wanting to be accepted by loved ones. Maybe it was loneliness I tucked away from my days in New Jersey or being touched by someone who didn't care about how much I weighed. Or maybe it was from staring at *Playboy* magazines wondering what it was all about. It could be all of the above. The bottom line is, it happened. I didn't know what a lesbian was. But I knew what I was doing was wrong.

This opened the door of my secret closet, a place where I would store the experiences that I wanted to hide from the world and myself. And that's precisely what I did. Stored it away and forgot it happened.

THE START OF RELATIONSHIPS

We met on the school bus, and I drove her nuts! But she was the coolest thing going. She carried confidence that made you want to be in her circle. I would always try to have conversations with her, but she blew me off. I appreciated her artistic flair and sense of humor. She was hysterical. One day on the bus ride home we realized we shared the same birthday one year apart, her being older. That got her attention, and we instantly became friends. She called me her "twin." The zodiac was a favorite way of deciphering life back then, so two Geminis born on the same date made us believe our souls were tied. We dove deeper into a friendship, and I eventually invited her to church with me. She came, along with a few of her friends. We talked about Jesus, the Bible, and life. We shared our dreams and visions about our future.

Faith and I both got cast in our high school's production of *Godspell*. *Godspell* not only drew me closer to Jesus, but it also drew me closer to her. This new friendship was more profound than any other relationship I've ever had. Faith was like a sister to me, someone who wanted to hang with me and know me—something I longed for. For the next two years of high school, we were locked into each other. I had other friends I hung out with, including a boyfriend, but Faith was my "person," and I knew I was hers. She wrote me letters of how special I was as a friend, and gave me books about life and told me how she loved me, but not in the "lesbian way."

My parents started getting suspicious of this friendship and how close we'd become. They were concerned. They found a box of letters from her that I stored away. I kept them hidden because they were so special to me. They ended up throwing the box away and questioning what this friendship was all about. This made them even question me going to church. They thought I was part of a cult. But I didn't think so. I went to our Catholic church every Tuesday night, studied the Bible, and had a close friend who understood who Jesus was. I don't blame them for being worried. They only knew of the Catholic Church as a typical mass and sacraments, while I was experiencing a charismatic version. But all the details of our relationship were getting tangled and caused confusion. There were warning signs my friend and I were becoming a bit too intimate—signs I was blinded by, and I'm sure she was too. But we had the same desires: intimacy.

I ended up finding intimacy with my first boyfriend, and I sensed the tension between my boyfriend and Faith but never understood it. They weren't fans of each other. So when my boyfriend and I lost our virginity to each other, she was there to pick up the broken pieces. That Tuesday night at church, Faith was who I turned to as a friend to help me cope with what I was feeling.

After a few years of our friendship, Faith opened up to me about being gay. I remember being shocked but filled with curiosity and questions. I didn't understand what that meant, or that it was a lifestyle. I certainly didn't let it affect our friendship. I did feel a sense of threat to our friendship, though, when she told me she was in love with a girl she had met. Somehow I thought I would be replaced and would lose my "soulmate." I never shared that with her, though. I kept it to myself and went off to college in Florida. We lost connection in my first year of college. She was off in the gay world, and I was doing my usual thing: trying to fit in somewhere. My old memories from New Jersey started turning into a new reality. I was alone.

I finally met my first real friend on the college campus. Cassie was a year older and a bit rough around the edges. Intimidating but super lovable. She was the cool cat on campus, and everyone loved her. I would notice her just like I noticed my best friend in high school. She was someone I aspired to be around, to be in her company. One day she started chatting with me, and we realized how much we had in common. Instantly, this turned into a deep friendship. Cassie and I hung out every day and became each other's "person."

Despite having found a friend, I was miserable in college and I wanted to quit and move back to Buffalo. My dad encouraged me to stick it out and get my degree. He told me to join some groups, maybe a sorority. I hated sororities. I saw their members all over campus in their jerseys. The girls were preppy, skinny, blonde, and pretty. The frat boys were cocky, arrogant, and really attractive. I avoided them at all costs. Soon enough my new friend Cassie showed up one day wearing a sorority jersey! I was shocked because she didn't fit the typical stereotype. In fact, none of the sisters in her sorority fit the mold. She brought me into her crew, and I finally started enjoying college. I decided to pledge, only because I loved the girls who were a part of our chapter, and I was initiated into the sorority. My bestie and I were inseparable during the second semester of my freshman year. It was comforting to know I had a friend who valued me and what I brought to the friendship table. So comforting, in fact, that we found ourselves lying in bed having heart-to-hearts about life, friendships, school, and the future. There was no attraction on either end, just companionship. She had a boyfriend who lived a few hours away, so she talked a lot about him. It felt normal to me, and we became a team. Everyone knew we were inseparable, but the "lesbian" title never even came to mind . . . until we kissed.

I powered through college until my first summer break when I flew home and stayed with my best friend from high school, Faith, in college dorm. It was more like a dorm apartment, and she shared it with a few other girls, including her girlfriend. I knew she was gay, so it didn't make any difference to me. I was just happy to be in her presence. I missed our coffee dates, our deep talks about life and the future, and how much we laughed together. But being in her dorm, I was immersed in the "gay" scene. This was her crew. She had a bunch of friends over, and we all had an evening of heavy drinking, board games, and spin the bottle. I kissed about eight girls that night, and we all had a bit too much to drink.

It was an evening I would never forget. As Faith and I were cleaning up her dorm room and catching up on life, we had a moment when our eyes locked in. I felt a pervasive sensation throughout my body, and I knew what was about to happen.

The first night I was intimate with her, I felt something shift inside. I didn't understand it, but it felt like the combination of passion and shame. My emotions were all over the place, and I sensed an obsession take over my mind. I couldn't be without her. I let her in, and she fulfilled every part of me. My best friend turned into my infatuation, and it took over my life. After spending an intimate week together, I had to head back to Florida. I cried the whole flight with mixed emotions and asked myself, *What did I just do?*

For this reason God gave them up to dishonorable passions. For their women exchanged natural relations for those that are contrary to nature; and the men likewise gave up natural relations with women and were consumed with passion for one another, men committing shameless acts with men and receiving in themselves the due penalty for their error. And since they did

not see fit to acknowledge God, God gave them up to a debased
mind to do what ought not to be done.   (Romans 1:26–28)

I have come to observe that homosexuality was not who I was but what I learned to be. I believe that is the same truth for anyone choosing this lifestyle. It starts with a desire. A desire to be loved. Period. To be accepted, touched, filled with a want, and to be needed and known. We all desire these things because God built us for desire. But when those desires become degrading in God's eyes, that's when it becomes sin.

The night I flew from Buffalo back to college in Florida was the night I confessed to Cassie that I kissed a girl. She didn't say a word for the entire forty-five-minute drive back to campus and just stared ahead at the road. She was the type who liked to process her thoughts but based on her silence I was worried she was judging me inside.

We buried the story and never talked about it again until the innocent jokes started between us. She'd whisper in my ear and jokingly accuse me of looking at another girl. I'd smack her on the arm and tell her to knock it off. But this became our secret joke to each other. I was still craving what I experienced in Buffalo, and she was starting to get curious to see what it was like. One night, we went out to the bar like all of us sorority sisters did and drank all night. We had a big frat party to attend later in the evening, but I forgot my wallet back in my room. She laid down on my bed because her head was spinning from the alcohol. So was mine and as I grabbed my wallet, I leaned down and gave her a peck on the lips. She opened her eyes and kissed me back.

For the next three years we dated in secret until we found out another one of our sorority sisters was also gay. We sat her down one evening and told her our story and the three of us protected each other. We all decided to move into an apartment off campus so that we could have more privacy. Cassie and I shared a room, and our friend had the other one by herself. Nobody ever questioned our living situation because we were the best of friends for so long. I loved Cassie, but my heart was growing complacent. It wasn't until I met a new girl on campus that caused a new flame to ignite in me.

She was loud and crazy, and we immediately hit it off and became instant friends. Her name was Hope and she was new to our school. Neither of us knew we were both gay, but we would soon come out to each other. In the past, every girl I was with was based on my close-knit friendship. But not this time. I was sexually attracted to her, more than I have ever been attracted to another girl. We had strong physical chemistry, and I couldn't fight it off any longer. We started seeing each other in secret, and my feelings were growing strong for her. But this fling didn't last long. I had to eventually break it off because I was burdened with guilt, my mind was in chaos, and my heart was confused. I felt like I was living in a warped world where nothing made sense. I was caught in a depraved web of cheating, lying, and sexual confusion.

Little did I know at the time that Hope would eventually be the person I would spend years with in a relationship and would almost marry.

I could go on and on and tell you details of how many times I broke up with one girlfriend to get back together with the other one, and vice versa. Or how I still made trips to Buffalo to see Faith. I could give you details on the guys I got physical with in college behind all of the girls' backs, but I am choosing to spare the details. The bottom line is this: I was handed over to a *depraved mind*. I was deep in sin and couldn't find my way out.

Now, after years of relearning my sexuality, I realize that I hurt so many people. I know we were all young and free to make our own choices, but my insecurities and confusions caused unnecessary pain to everyone I came in contact with. As I was trying to figure out who I was, they were all getting dragged through my mud. I had a void in my life, and I chose to fill it with a counterfeit version of love. The enemy of God sniffed me out and one by one he took us all down. Satan's stronghold was passed down to the next victim. I believe that each and every girl I was with is still living the homosexual life. That's why I chose to keep them anonymous. I love and care for each of them dearly, and they are part of my life story.

Hope and I ended up getting together again after college. She became my constant companion, which is all I really wanted. Someone to be by my side through thick and thin. She was there when I went after my dreams in Nashville and LA, and she was there when I gave them up. She supported me every step of the way.

After many years of living in secret, I decided to empty all the intimate skeletons in my closet and come out to my parents. It was one of the most difficult things I have ever done. It hurt to say the words to them because I knew it was a lie. But it was my "reality" and I chose to stay in it. I chose to believe I was born that way and I had no intention of changing. I chose to believe what the world was dictating to me—that because I kissed a girl I must be gay. This was my fate, so it was time to come clean.

I remember sitting on the front step of my apartment smoking a cigarette. I called my mom to talk to her about the details of my sister's wedding, and we got into an argument which led me to finally telling her the truth. As the words came out of my mouth, time stood still, and for a moment I wished I could grab the words out of thin air and put them back into my mouth. But they were out. And I was finally out. My parents didn't take it very well, and we didn't speak for a few weeks. We finally decided to have dinner and talk through it. As I sat at the kitchen table, my mom was behind me banging pots and pans as she was cooking and my father sat across from me. He went on to say that he didn't understand and that both he and my mom weren't raised in a generation that accepted this, but I was their daughter and they both loved me very much. My mom, God bless her, was so angry she told me to get back in the closet! I laugh about it now but back then it was heartbreaking for all of us. I felt like I was trying to convince them to believe a lie. I remember feeling so disconnected and wishing this never happened to me. But at the same time, I had strong feelings for my girlfriend and didn't know how to justify it.

Eventually, we all moved on from the conversation and never spoke of it again, until one Christmas when I decided to challenge my family and chose to spend Christmas with my girlfriend and her family. To my surprise, my mom offered to do our family Christmas a day early to accommodate me. I have to be honest and tell you that it made me feel so sad that I forced my parents to accept the way I was choosing to live. I felt their love, but I also felt their disappointment. I think they both decided to let me figure this one out and that one day I would come around to the truth.

They say that mothers know their daughters well, just like fathers have a deep connection with their sons. I think that's the reason my mom and I fought so much for the next few years. She knew I wasn't being true to who I was. She was frustrated as any mom would be watching her child head down the wrong road. I felt shameful every time I was around them, not because of them, but because of me.

I hate dealing with shame in my life, and the more I had, the heavier it got. I finally realized I couldn't do anything with it. I couldn't fight it or get rid of it. I could've passed it on to other people, but that added more shame. I was stuck with the shame until Jesus relieved me of it. As much as I hate shame, it's the very thing that opened me back up to His love.

CHAPTER 7

Identity Crisis

It was June 2007, the month of my thirtieth birthday. I took a mental note of my messy twenties and had hope for a better decade. Hope was planning a getaway and invited a bunch of my friends to come along. I was looking forward to getting away and celebrating my birthday with my people but one by one they canceled. We were left with just the two of us.

She arranged a beautiful weekend getaway in Canada. We had lots of fun activities planned, including dinner at a Brazilian steakhouse. It's the type of restaurant where the servers roam the floor with skewers full of various types of meat. Each person gets a little coaster with green on one side and red on the other. If you want more meat, keep the green side visible. If you're done with your meat course, turn it to red and they will leave you alone.

We were ready to stuff ourselves and that's exactly what we did. She was acting a little off and I couldn't tell if something was bothering her but I chose to ignore it. We finally had our fill of meat and flipped the cards over to red. Our server came over asking if we wanted more. I was confused because my card was flipped over to red but responded that I was all set and super full. He proceeded to ask me again if I wanted more but this time he said, "How about having some of this?" As the words were coming out of his mouth he placed the tip of an empty skewer on my plate and slowly lowered a diamond ring onto the surface. Shocked, I looked up at Hope and she asked, "Will you marry me, Keri?"

REALITY HITS

It's all fun and games until someone gets hurt, or until you realize it's gone on for way too long.

My life from age sixteen up until I turned thirty was all about doing what I wanted without much accountability. I jumped from one relationship to the next. If one didn't work out, we would break up and get back together a few times until we couldn't make it work anymore. But in every homosexual relationship I was in, I could never give it 100 percent. I would go 80 percent but left room for error. I never realized I felt that way until I was faced with a proposal from someone who loved me with her whole heart. I loved her but not enough to commit my life to her. This decision was not a criticism of her as a person, but more of a criticism of what our relationship represented. After I came out to my family and to the rest of the world, I had no problem stating that I was gay, but deep down inside I couldn't give my full heart to it. Something would hold me back.

There were many nights I would lie in bed next to my girlfriend and have silent prayer wars with God. My life never felt quite right. I would ask Him where He went or why He left me. I would cry out that something felt wrong in my life but that

I didn't know how to fix it or to even pinpoint what the problem was. When I didn't get a response, I would just cover my head with the blanket and hopelessly fall asleep.

My girlfriend knew I battled with my faith, and she did as well. So it was a familiar topic that came up from time to time. Many churches in the area were gay-friendly so we would attempt to attend, but they didn't feel right either. It felt like the people were there, but Jesus wasn't. We would discuss the level of our faith and that we both desired more, but at the end of the day, our relationship won and God would be put on the backburner.

I always wondered what my life would be like if I weren't dating a girl. I'd play scenes in my head with certain guys I liked from my past but quickly realized none of them could be trusted. I always had a fear of being emotionally hurt by a guy based on how things turned out with my first boyfriend in high school. My girlfriend could be trusted, though. I knew without a shadow of a doubt that she loved me. I loved her too, but there was a part of me that was holding back. She was my companion and I felt safe with her, just like I did with every other girl I was with.

EMOTIONAL SECURITY

As women, when it comes to being relationally involved with another human being, I firmly believe underneath our tough exteriors we ultimately want to be protected and cared for. We have the genuine need to be secure. We need to know we are safe and well provided for in every aspect, even if that means taking matters into our own hands. For me, emotional safety hits the top of that list, with being provided for in second place.

My whole life I watched women take on the strength and protection roles that should have been handled by a man.

My father's parents were very different from my mother's parents but I saw similarities. It started by watching how both of my grandmothers took the lead role in their households. Unfortunately, my two grandfathers were war veterans and both struggled with PTSD along with other vices. They also had their own histories—one being raised in Italy and trained to fend for himself, and the other raised as an orphan and trained to feel like he never belonged to anyone. I believe these things caused instability which is why my grandmothers became the pillars in their homes. I loved and respected both of my grandfathers as any grandchild would—God rest their hurting souls—but the older I got and the more stories I heard, the more I understood how this created a line of strong, self-sufficient women in our family whose main goal was survival. Both of my grandmothers have passed and I believe they are finally resting. But they have passed down the strength torch to all the girls to carry.

My parents were different, though. They worked together to raise me, my sister, and my brother. My father worked to provide for us and my mother worked by staying at home to raise us. Some would call her a stay-at-home mom who didn't work, but she worked her tail off to take care of us, so we like to say she was the General Manager of the Cardinale household! Both of their efforts provided for a loving home. We were well taken care of and provided with basic needs and beyond. I wouldn't say we were spoiled, but most likely we were. I think it's because my parents were raised with next to nothing.

To this day, I have never worried about being provided for. I have been in many ruts in my life and every time, without question or fail, my parents were there to catch me. They have always provided a safety net for me while I was figuring out who I was and where I was going. They offer the same net for my sister and brother. This doesn't mean they always dished out money, although they have helped me out of a few stupid financial jams in my twenties, for which I am grateful. I always have a sense of security that no matter where I land in life, there is always a home for me to rest my head at my parents' house. I have many fears but I never fear that I'm going to be in financial despair. Somehow they embedded a comfort in me to know that I will always be provided for. Because of this, I am able to trust that God will always provide for me.

I was raised in a loving household, but certainly not a quiet one. We are not a quiet family and our neighbors knew it. My sister and I fought like wild banshees and so did my parents. My brother was born when I was thirteen years old so he grew up witnessing it all. I think that's why he's the most even-keeled out of all of us. He flees from conflict and wants nothing to do with it, unless his buttons push him to the point of insanity! We push buttons well in the Cardinale family. My parents fought like any normal married couple, though, and they never involved us. We never heard our names being called out in the midst of their arguments but we felt the hostility between them. I would sit outside their bedroom door praying for them to stop while my sister went to her room and put her headphones on. My brother walked away as well. They both removed themselves while I stayed close. I couldn't sleep until I knew they were okay.

I wasn't around to see how both my parents handled their own upbringings but I can only imagine how volatile it was for them. They both witnessed women taking the lead and fighting for survival. As much as I knew my parents were protecting me physically, I never trusted that anyone was protecting me emotionally. I became self-sufficient in protecting my heart, which caused me to hold it under lock and key.

TO BE UNDERSTOOD

My need to be understood went from desire to demand. I became the girl who demanded respect from every man I came into contact with, whether it was my teacher, a potential boyfriend, or my boss. I wanted to be on an equal playing field and challenged them in every way that I knew how. I came to understand this was just one big wall I built using my emotional survival skills. But I didn't know how to knock the wall down, or to even drill a hole so that the men could attempt to get close to me. All I knew was that no man was going to tell me what to do, how to live, how to love, or when to do the laundry—unless he respected me. The only way I could tell if he respected me was if he put me on a pedestal. There were only two men in my life that I respected. One was (and is) my dad, who celebrated my wins and put each of us kids on a pedestal; the other was Father Francis Pompei.

Father Pompei was my teacher in high school for just a short time but he carried a light with him that couldn't be turned off. He operated in truth and integrity, mixed with compassion and the most beautiful display of Jesus' love here on earth. He was relevant, funny, real, and completely sure of his identity. He had such a genuine love for us girls that we couldn't help but want to be around him. Father Pompei also had a love for the arts and a passion for bringing the mystery of Christ's birth to life. He created a meditational play called the "Franciscan Mystery Play" with few speaking parts. The only voices you heard were of one or two adults who gave different reflections on the scenes. But the actors were all teens. Father Pompei called them the "mystery players" who played out the scenes leading up to Jesus' birth with background music and mood lighting. It was the most beautiful and powerful display of truth I had ever witnessed and made me fall in love with Jesus even more.

Father Pompei and I had so many talks about life, faith, and Jesus. So naturally all I wanted to do my senior year was to be a mystery player. It was a small group of ten to twelve students from our all-girl high school and boys from a local all-boy high school. So you can imagine my surprise when I didn't get the part! I was shocked. I thought for sure I was a shoe-in. I was known not only for my role in *Godspell*, but also for my intense love for Jesus— which was slightly unheard of in our school.

Father Pompei wrapped his arm around me and pulled me in close. He was a Franciscan friar which meant little or no deodorant! But I didn't care when he stood close to me; I figured Jesus didn't wear deodorant either so I was in good company. He encouraged me that there was only one reason why he didn't give me a role in the play.

Our high school was putting on the production of *Cinderella* around the same time the *Mystery Play* would be traveling to different churches. A few months before auditioning for the play, I auditioned for the lead role as Cinderella and landed the Fairy Godmother. I was super disappointed because I wanted the leading role for my last year of high school, but the truth is, I wasn't Cinderella material! I wish that I was, but the girl who got the role fit perfectly into a sparkled gown with her hourglass figure, big chest, and beautiful blonde hair. I fit the Fairy Godmother role perfectly! I was bubbly, chubby, loud, and expressive with my singing voice. I wasn't dainty like a princess, I was bouncy and boisterous like a fairy godmother. I didn't like this really, so I decided that I could do more good in the *Mystery Play*.

Father Pompei said, "Keri, you belong on the big stage where you can sing your heart out. I didn't choose you, but it's for your own good. You may not see that now, but you will soon enough. I want you to shine up there and be seen for your incredible gifts." This meant so much to me. He even agreed to make stage props with lights under my cape and smoke to go off when I turned the pumpkin into a carriage. I decided to play the role of Fairy Godmother, and it was a huge success! As for the *Mystery Play*, I enjoyed going to as many churches as I could to support the team and to connect with Jesus by watching His story come alive.

Father Pompei put me on a pedestal when I didn't believe I deserved to be up there. Not only did he root for me, but he gave me the tools to succeed, just like my dad. I learned at that age what real love and respect felt like. But after a few random encounters with high school boys and how they treated me, it quickly got rerouted and my walls started to go up. Year after year, more walls were built until my definition of love and respect became distorted.

LOVE AND RESPECT

However, let each one of you love his wife as himself, and let the wife see that she respects her husband. (Ephesians 5:33)

Yikes. This Scripture knows how to stir up trouble. I was sitting in church a few years back when my pastor spoke about women in the church and their roles as wives. I sat in the choir as a single girl surrounded by some revved up married ladies. I learned quickly that in some Christian communities this Scripture is frowned upon. I heard a few ladies murmur under their breath, "My husband better respect me!" I was still in my camp of "You respect me or else there'll be trouble" so I could understand their frustration. But I had never heard this Scripture before so I was curious what the deeper meaning was. In fact, I was hoping for a deeper meaning, or this pastor was going to get drop kicked! He proceeded to read other verses from the book of Ephesians:

> *Wives, submit to your own husbands, as to the Lord. For the husband is the head of the wife even as Christ is the head of the church, his body, and is himself its Savior. Now as the church submits to Christ, so also wives should submit in everything to their husbands.*
>
> *Husbands, love your wives, as Christ loved the church and gave himself up for her, that he might sanctify her, having cleansed her by the washing of water with the word, so that he might present the church to himself in splendor, without spot or wrinkle or any such thing, that she might be holy and without blemish. In the same way husbands should love their wives as their own bodies. He who loves his wife loves himself.*
> (Ephesians 5:22–28)

As the Scriptures were showing up on the screen, I started to sense my mind churning. Scenes from my past began playing and I thought of how my dad adored my mom. I used to love when they would go out for the evening when I was a kid. My dad would put on a suit and tie, and my mom would dress up in a pretty black dress or black suit with sparkling jewelry. She'd be in the bathroom spraying her blonde hair and then apply her makeup at the vanity mirror in her room. She had about twenty different tubes of red lipstick and a drawer filled with foundation, blush, and mascara. I remember my mom would paint a quick coat of nail polish at the kitchen table, they'd both spritz cologne and perfume, give us a kiss goodbye, and head out. My favorite times were when they would bring us home leftover wedding cake or bring home a pizza for their late night snack. The smell of pepperoni, peppers, and onions made its way up to my bedroom then I'd hear my dad call us down to eat with them. I knew my mom and dad loved and respected each other, but when I thought about this verse, I realized, yes, my dad loves my mom. He gave her gifts, dressed her up and took her out, and always talked about how much he loved her. He cherished her. My mom was the love of his life and still is. And my mom respected my dad. She understood him and supported him as they continued to build our family foundation.

I recalled Father Pompei and even though he wasn't my "husband," he operated in a loving way similar to how Christ loves the church. He provided solid leadership when my emotions were trying to run the show. And he brought out the best in me and encouraged me to play the role of Fairy Godmother.

These Scriptures helped to soften my heart toward men. God's Word is actually the only thing I can give credit to when it comes to my transformation. It has touched every area of my life and reset my deep misunderstandings. The Bible, when taken at face value, may seem harsh and scary, and sometimes very difficult to interpret. But I promise you if you give God a chance to use His words to speak truth into your heart, you will be blown away just like I was and still am every time I read it.

These eight verses found in Ephesians changed my life. I had a revelation that day on the choir platform while the women around me whispered about how their husbands needed to respect them. I sat there and dreamed about what could be and had my own private conversation with God thanking Him for His truth. And the truth is I am just a girl who wants to be loved at the end of the day. I want a man to go "all out" for me and shower me with flowers and gifts! How wonderful it would be to hear words of affirmation on a daily basis that build me up and words that bring out the best in me. I'll take a man that can get rid of spots and wrinkles! Add holiness and blemish free and we've got a deal! God, you are telling me this is how a husband ought to love his wife? Sign me up! What do I have to do to prepare myself for this husband?

That was the day I let my guard down and admitted to myself that this is the kind of love I've always desired. For years I tried to make myself believe that I wasn't interested in men and that the love I received from a woman was better, sweeter, and, honestly, safer. But it was a lie. A woman can do the same things for me— all the attributes described in Ephesians—but it's not the same. I received flowers and affirming words from my ex-girlfriends and they were all wonderful gestures, but they never made my heart beat the way they do now when I receive them from a man.

This new revelation shifted my heart in other areas too, including ministry and the workplace. I began to allow myself to be a woman in a man's world. I hung up my black power suits and traded them in for soft colors. This doesn't mean I believed I deserved less than what I was worth as a career woman. In fact, this new truth set me free to believe in what I had to offer. I decided to come alongside men instead of competing with them. When I stopped demanding respect in the workplace, my superiors started to see what I was really capable of. You see, I had built walls around my heart that portrayed a tough exterior, ultimately to protect myself from being rejected. I finally found the root and realized it was causing me issues in more than just my sexuality—it affected every area of my life. I was blocking my own potential. I came out from behind the walls and became the girl Father Pompei saw, a girl capable of doing anything she set her mind to. I just had to stop fighting. I had to surrender. When I fell into the natural order that God created for me, it all changed.

FEMININITY

Just as security and being understood are our greatest needs as women, intimacy and connection are our greatest desires. After coming to conclusions about my dysfunctional relationship with men, I needed to understand my attraction to women. I've always been attracted to women for as long as I can remember but for more reasons that you would assume.

I'll start with the sexual attraction. This began at a young age when my eyes gazed at that *Playboy* magazine. After having my first sexual encounter with a woman, my childhood *Playboy* story would come up in conversations. Some people would say I was gay because I was fixated on the woman in the magazine. I thought I was too, until I gave my story more attention. The truth is, I wanted to be the woman who the guy was drooling over! I was attracted to her response and desired to have the same experience. I was sexually aroused by the act. It's like I was imagining what it's like to have her body. I thought I was attracted to her but the truth is I wanted to be her. I thought I stared at women in the magazines because I was attracted to women, but this was a lie that I believed for many years until the Lord showed me the truth.

Women are naturally beautiful. Our skin, hair, and other features were created to be soft and appealing, and our bodies created to be attractive and beautiful to men, whether we believe these things about ourselves or not. I never really believed I was beautiful or appealing to the eye. I would see girls in elementary school, high school, college, and even now, and I pick out their natural beauty. I'd want their long pretty hair, or skinny bodies. I wish I had their hairless face and perfect skin. For years this view got distorted and I confused envy with attraction. I thought since I looked at girls and scanned their beauty that I was attracted to them. I assumed the same-sex attraction meant I was a lesbian. Now that I see the truth, I am able to appreciate and celebrate the beauty of myself and other women.

When two people look into each other's eyes, they are recognizing something familiar in the other person. I was emotionally attracted to women and they were emotionally attracted to me. I loved to be nurtured and cared for, and women do this well. I yearned to be connected to someone I could trust and I trusted women. But when I allowed certain friendships to develop on a more intimate level, lines were crossed. Once this line is crossed it's very difficult to turn back. We all have those female friends who satisfy us in many ways. We can be ourselves and laugh for hours. Female friends are great for coffee dates, shopping sprees, and swapping gluten-free recipes. We mourn losses with one another and celebrate when good things happen. We also rely on each other when we just need a shoulder to cry or an ear to vent it out. But when boundaries aren't placed in a friendship of two emotionally hungry women searching for love, security, and connection, you could run into a problem. I did, and I have seen and heard of many women—single or married, churched or unchurched—who find their anchor in another woman. This anchor can eventually lead to a sexual encounter.

I have come to understand my relationships in the past with women and I now have boundaries. Not because I'm afraid I'll go back to that way of life, but more because I don't ever want to rely on another woman for that type of intimate, emotional fulfillment. I spent the last decade of my life learning about what went wrong in my earlier years and how to move forward in healthy relationships. I have found that if I need to be fulfilled in those areas so bad that I turn to a woman, then something is off in my relationship with the Lord. He ultimately fulfills me and I am satisfied in Him. Whatever I get from my female friends now and my husband is all a bonus.

PROPOSAL

The moment Hope asked me to marry her, I felt the world stop spinning. Imagine a movie where the actor breaks the fourth wall. That's when they talk directly to the camera about the scene you are about to watch. It's as if the movie stops for a moment while the character talks to you, the audience.

It was three seconds. Everyone in that Brazilian steakhouse stopped moving and breathing for three seconds while I broke the fourth wall and spoke to God. I cried out...

God, I need your help.

In those three seconds of time and space, my desperate words rumbled the universe and rippled their way into the throne room of God. He heard my cry.

> *Before they call I will answer; while they are yet speaking I will hear.* (Isaiah 65:24)

In those three seconds, I realized something was wrong in my heart. God was waiting, very patiently, for me to come to this realization on my own. A thousand people could have told me my self-made sexual identity was outside of God's will for my life but I wouldn't have listened. It was fulfilling every unfulfilled area of my life. But the moment I questioned it—the moment I acknowledged I needed God's help—was the moment He heard me.

> *We know that God does not listen to sinners, but if anyone is a worshiper of God and does his will, God listens to him.*
>
> (John 9:31)

This was the beginning of my rescue mission.

PAINFUL LOSS

To save face I said yes. I put the ring on my finger and servers ran over with a bottle of champagne. While everyone in the restaurant was cheering, I was dying inside. Beyond my sadness, I was worried about my girlfriend. I knew I wanted out and I knew it was going to break her heart. But I felt trapped. Walking away meant giving up everything I've known and everything I stood for. All the truths that I trained my heart to believe about myself were going to be torn away.

We left Niagara Falls and headed back to Buffalo. As I stared at the ring on my finger I knew my life was about to change. Either I was going to be married to a woman or we were about to embark on the pain of our world—the world we created together—falling apart. But we got home, resumed life as normal, and I came to terms with the engagement. Within a few months after my birthday weekend, however, we started arguing a lot. I don't know why we were fighting so much but somehow we were on two separate wavelengths. I started to sense a distance from her so I questioned if she wanted to still get married. She opened up to me about having feelings for another girl. As much as it hurt, I listened to her as a best friend would. I've been in this spot before—having feelings for someone while we were together—so I didn't judge her for it. I just listened. She was confused about her feeling so I encouraged her to take time to figure it out. But after a week of no contact I started to panic. In the past, I would have fought to keep her but this time something was different. I saw a way out. Not out from her as a person, but out from the life I was living. She finally admitted that she wanted to be with the other girl so I graciously let her go. This closed the chapter of our ten-year relationship.

The next month was rough. It was the end of August 2007 and I was not only going through a breakup but also studying for my finals in Massage Therapy. Three days after we broke up I got an unexpected email from an old cyber-pal. His name was Grant and he lived on the other side of the world.

CHAPTER 8

A Beautiful Distraction

A good friend at work asked me if I was going to keep dating women now that my girlfriend and I broke up, or would I go back to men? I answered, "Neither." I didn't know who I was anymore or what I wanted... until a few days later when I met Grant.

Grant was from Scotland and we connected years back on a social media platform. We had innocent conversations about a band we both loved, and the conversations lasted only a few weeks. So it was refreshing when I received an email from him three days after my girlfriend and I broke up. But this time he wasn't just calling as a friend. He told me he was going through his old contacts and his heart skipped a beat when he came across my picture, so he had to connect with me again. My tears suddenly dried up and I was very intrigued.

It happened fast but we fell madly in love with each other. Well, we thought it was love. It was more of a virtual love. I have never had a man open up to me as much as he did, and I opened up to him. We became each other's comfort. We chatted day and night, night and day. I lived at home with my parents at the time because I was in school full time studying for my Massage Therapy license and working full time. So every chance I had I'd hunker down in my dad's den and talk with Grant on Skype. We were engrossed with each other and he became the main focus of my world. I never thought I could feel this way about a man but he was different. He was kind and affectionate with his words toward me. He called me "darling" and calmed my spirit.

I've always been the adventurous type, so naturally I booked a flight with a few friends and flew five thousand miles to Scotland to meet face to face. It was February 2008 and we landed safely in Edinburgh. It wasn't as easy back then as it is now to communicate by phone with someone overseas, so I prayed he was going to be at the spot we said we would meet.

There he was. Grant in the flesh. This man who stole my heart in a matter of two weeks. The man who stole my attention away from women, and the one who gave me hope that I was worthy to be loved by a man. I often wonder if God allows distractions to help us prepare for what's to come. That's how I would describe my relationship with Grant.

He welcomed me with a big hug and a bouquet of flowers. But as much as I felt connected to him in my heart, I felt disconnected in person. I know he did too, so it took us the day to get reacquainted with each other.

We spent the whole week together in a flat we all rented in downtown Edinburgh. He took me to meet his mom, and showed me all of his favorite places around town. And yes, we were intimate with each other. We talked about marriage and how we were going to settle our lives down in Scotland. He'd come to Buffalo to meet my family in a few months, then I'd move there. I wasn't sure how we were going to survive because he was a struggling musician and I was a massage therapist, but we trusted it was all going to work out. I gave him a kiss at the airport and said, "I'll see you soon in Buffalo." Then I flew home. Little did I know that was the beginning of the end. The next five months consisted of making plans and breaking plans. He was waiting on his passport and I was starting to wonder if he'd ever come see me.

Grant and I became each other's savior. He was a loner for a long time and never got over the death of his father. He lived with his mom and didn't have many friends. He used to call me his "angel" and say that if there was a God, he was grateful God sent me to him. I loved caring for his emotions and I loved being needed. I felt like he was a gift too. He showed me that it was possible to love and be loved by a man. Once I had that, I never wanted to let it go. We clung to each other five thousand miles apart.

Grant wasn't a believer; in fact, he claimed to be an atheist. He knew that I loved Jesus, though. I would share with him about how I knew Jesus when I was younger and how I was still searching for Him. But I wasn't there yet, so my "religion" became the love Grant and I had for each other. I continued to wait for him to come and see me but I was growing impatient. I started questioning if he even wanted to come, but he continued to reassure me that his passport was on hold.

In the meantime, I sensed something else nudging me.

GOD WHISPERS

Many people don't know this about me, but at one point I was studying to be a psychic. Years ago I got caught up in a group of people who were very open to all different types of spirits and rituals. For five years I attended retreats on their land a few hours from Buffalo. I did silent retreats, cleansing retreats, vision retreats, and peace weekends. We'd spend hours in the meditation room in front of a Buddhist statue in full lotus position. The room was filled with framed pictures of other spiritual leaders from around the world, including a picture of Jesus. I always felt at ease when I saw this picture. The people were wonderful and so kind. They respected the entire human race, animals, insects, and spirits. I learned how to eat well and how to keep my anxiety and depression to a minimum. I got so involved in the process of healing that I became a level 2 Reiki practitioner. Reiki is a spiritual practice that supposedly activates and directs mystical energies. I wanted to be a source of healing for people, so I figured this was an option to offer. The danger of this practice is that I allowed myself to be open to familiar spirits. I had to be initiated by one of the Reiki "masters." During my attunement ceremony, the master traced ancient symbols on my head, and then on other places on my body, known as the chakras. This process is supposed to open up energy sources so that I can transfer positive energy to other people. I know, sounds sacrilegious. But this is what searching for your faith looks like. You go the distance to find it.

I tried everything I could to find inner healing with the group. From urine therapy to four-hour sweat lodges, I was committed to finding something that resembled my old faith. I remember a moment I had on a silent retreat. I was in silence for four days straight. I thought I would break silence but I didn't. The problem wasn't the no-talking part. It was the voices in my head that I couldn't shut down. Sometimes we sat through the sessions in the meditation room and sometimes we went outside for walking meditations. These weren't normal walks, though. They were super slow with thought-out steps. One foot at a time. One day on our walk we had to create a mantra to repeat over and over again. I wanted to be okay with believing in all types of religions so I started to chant a list. "It's okay to believe in Buddhism, it's okay to believe in Hinduism, it's okay to believe in paganism... It's okay to believe in Jesus." I would start to tear up every time I said His name. It's like my heart knew it belonged to Him and I grieved putting Jesus in a category with other religions.

Since I was studying to be a psychic, my best friend and I went to a psychic fair in April 2008. I had a few readings done but I felt like something was off. I turned to my friend and said, "I think I want to learn about Jesus again." I felt a shift in the air that day. Before I even understood Romans 8:28: *"And we know that for those who love God all things work together for good, for those who are called according to his purpose."* I was walking it out. That day at the psychic fair I met a woman. She was a nurse practitioner who was promoting natural hormone therapy and weight loss. I took her card because I was desperate for help and saved it in my wallet so that I wouldn't forget to call her.

In the meantime, my friend and I went to the bookstore so that I could find a book about Jesus. I found a few that had different titles and couldn't decide which one to buy until I saw book that just had the name "Jesus" on the cover. That was the one, so we made our purchases and went on with our day. I never actually read the book but I carried it around with me wherever

I went. It was like a long-lost souvenir reminding me of a distant memory. It seemed that ever since that day I started to see signs of God in different places. I would be at a meeting and someone would mention the Bible. Or something would come on the radio about church. I would see things that reminded me of Jesus and my curiosity was sparked. I wanted to attempt church again but never made it there. I would share these experiences with Grant but every time I brought up anything about Jesus, God, or my faith, he would either shut it down or challenge me on the topic. This would always lead to an argument and I was starting to feel unsure about our relationship. I couldn't bear the idea of losing him so I would cool down the arguments and move the conversation on to other things like, "So, how was your day?"

He finally got his passport and purchased his plane ticket to come to Buffalo, but I was feeling uneasy about Grant coming and I wanted to lose some weight before he got there, so I pulled out the business card of the holistic nurse practitioner I met at the psychic fair a few months back and made an appointment. It was July 4, 2008, when I sat in her office and opened up about my current state of depression. I shared with her my situation with Grant and how I was starting to not trust him. I talked to her about my work situation in a medical office and wondering if I should consider going back to school to study a higher profession in the medical field. She was gracious with me and listened to every one of my concerns. She asked me what I really wanted to do with my life. I said, "I know this will sound crazy, but I think I want to be a Christian singer!" She asked, "Are you even a Christian?" I said, "No, not really. I used to go to church when I was younger, but I haven't been in a long time."

I've always loved Christian music. In fact, my best friend reminded me that when we used to drive back and forth to Nashville when we lived there together, I would write Christian songs on the drive home. When I lived in LA, I wrote a song about being connected to my soul. It sounds New Age but that was the only way I knew how to explain the faith I desired to have back in my life. I remember driving and hearing a gospel-like song on the radio about believing that God could move mountains and that He was forever true and faithful. This song caught my attention so I looked it up when I got home and learned it was by the artist Rita Springer. I downloaded the song and burned it on a CD. It landed right in the middle of all my electronic dance music! I did a search for more of her songs and found myself listening to her music more than anything else. I started searching for other Christian songs and found some dance remixes form artists like Rebecca St. James. This was the beginning of my Christian music collection and it's the music that inspired me to answer my nurse practitioner's question.

She asked me if I was interested in going to church and wanted to make a recommendation. Since I'd been searching for a while, I welcomed it. She started to describe this church as one that I would connect with, mainly because of the music. I went home and looked it up online and immediately felt intimidated. It took me a few weeks but I finally got the courage to go on July 13, 2008. It was a big church and seated about 2,500 people. You can imagine how overwhelmed I felt. But I took a seat and was ready to be taught something new.

The music definitely got my attention, but it was the message that I heard that made the most impact. The church was in the middle of a series called "Olympic Moment," and the pastor's message was titled "The Refining Pot for Silver." I got lost a bit as we were reading through Scriptures but at certain moments he got my attention. The pastor was describing what happens to silver when it hits the melting pot. As it's being crushed, the impurities, or the gunk, rises to the top and the silver looks very unattractive for a while. Just like when God brings trials into our lives and we get angry and frustrated. But God allows these ugly traits to come to the surface so that we can acknowledge them for the sake of purifying our faith and making our hearts genuine.

I started to think about my relationship with Grant. We were having a lot of issues, so I found myself asking God what He was trying to expose in me. I started to think about my depression, which led me to think about my whole life. "God, I feel like You are trying to show me something but I don't know what." I started to wonder if He'd been trying to show me things all along, but I just ignored it. The pastor asked the final question, "Are you willing to submit to the purification process, stay under it to allow the impurities to rise up, and then allow God to accomplish His good purpose in your life?" I said nothing out loud but inside I was screaming yes.

I left church that day feeling refreshed and excited to hear more. I called up a friend of mine and asked her if she wanted to go to church with me the following Sunday. She was one of my ex-girlfriends who I've remained friends with after the years and she agreed to go. I could tell she felt uncomfortable, making statements like, "If they only knew I was gay!" and, "I'm surprised I haven't burned the place down yet!"

The service started and a choir was on the platform. I hadn't experienced a choir since my high school chorus class! I loved that class, so seeing the choir gave me a familiar feeling. A woman stepped out on stage with a microphone in her hand and began to lead the choir in a song.

As the song progressed so did the energy on the stage and in the room. The blended voices of different harmonies were singing out, "Hallelujah!" I could feel the energy in my body and I couldn't help but stand up. I didn't open my mouth to sing, but my heart was singing so loud inside. My friend never went back to church, but that day I decided I wanted to be a part of that choir.

Two months later I decided to join the choir. I went in that day and was asked to sing a song as an audition. I picked "Amazing Grace" because I didn't really know any other church songs. The three pastors I auditioned for were very encouraging to me and said nice things about my voice. Soon after, I walked into the choir room with my friend from work who thought she might want to join as well. I was so glad she was with me because I felt super out of place. I remember looking around and thinking, *I don't want to be friends with anyone here. I just want to sit in the back and get the rust off my vocal cords.*

The last time I opened my mouth to sing was five years prior when I moved back home from LA. I gave up on my dream of ever using my voice for something great. No song felt right to sing. Music became very empty to me—until the day I heard the choir sing. My first day in choir gave me hope that I could learn to sing a new type of song, one that would bring me joy and allow others to experience the same joy, just like how the choir inspired me.

I ended up loving my first day at rehearsal and couldn't wait to go back. My friend, not so much, so I was on my own from this point on. It was time to meet new people. Two women sat at the front of the alto section so they invited me to join them. We became the best of friends and they took me under their wing. I was grateful because I felt lost in the big church.

Choir brought me so much joy in such a short amount of time. It's what brought me into the church, but Grant was not happy about it at all. He was already bothered by my recent curiosity with Jesus, and once I joined choir he started to question if God was getting in the way of our relationship. We battled through every spiritual argument you can think of. Whenever I shared my thoughts about the Lord or about what I was learning, he would find a way to challenge it. I hated fighting with him because I loved him so much and I assured him that I wouldn't become one of those crazy Bible-beating Christian fanatics, so I started to downplay what I was learning every Sunday. But I stood my ground about joining choir. I tried to invite him to watch me in choir online for the live Internet feed but he would give excuses for why he couldn't watch it. I thought if maybe he caught some of the message it would change his mind, but he saw through my motives. I still couldn't wait to talk every day but it bothered me that I couldn't share this new part of my life with him.

A few weeks after I joined choir, the worship pastor approached me and pulled me aside. He shared with me that the team has been praying about introducing a new song to the congregation and that they've been waiting for the right person to come along to sing it. It was a pretty big gospel song and even though I was new to the group, they believed I was capable of delivering it Sunday morning. So they asked me to pray about it.

The whole worship scene was very new to me. I wasn't raised in a church that had a "worship leader." We had a choir, an organist, and maybe a flute from time to time. If there ever was a solo, it was the organist who sang it. There was never a spotlight or attention drawn to the singer, either. In the parish I grew up in, the organist was high up in the balcony facing the opposite way of the altar. He had to use a mirror to watch when the priest was ready to sing the offertory chant. I never experienced a church with lights, cameras, and a smoke machine. I thought it was all really cool, but it was just very different from what I knew. To be honest, I never knew what worship was. I knew how to sing and how to sing church songs but I didn't realize church songs were about worshiping God. I guess I always had it in my heart to do it because I would tell people I wanted to be a Christian singer. My goal was to encourage people with positive music. I never thought that I could be someone to motivate a congregation to worship God and prepare their hearts to hear the Word of God. I can only assume the pastors who approached me to sing the song saw this potential in me when I didn't even understand the responsibility I would soon be carrying.

Honestly, I didn't even know what they meant when they said, "Pray about it." I was still trying to wrap my brain around the first message I ever heard at the church about being refined like silver. I had a boyfriend who lived in a foreign country five thousand miles away who was an atheist. He would be in Buffalo in a few weeks and I was trying to come up with a plan on how to get him to go to church with me. I joined choir to find joy in the art of singing again and I still wasn't sure if this was where I belonged. At this point, I'd been attending church for only two months and just joined choir a few weeks back. These people didn't know anything about me. They didn't know that I was addicted to cigarettes. They had no clue that I lost my faith years ago and still felt disconnected. And they didn't know that for fifteen years I was a lesbian.

When I joined choir I had to fill out a card so they could gather more information about me. My answers were vague, not because I wanted to lie to anyone, but because I didn't really understand the questions and how to answer them. Some of the questions were "When were you saved?" and "Were you ever baptized?" The truth is, I felt inadequate to not only be part of the choir but part of the church. I asked myself, *Was I even a Christian?* I wanted to be, but I wasn't convinced that I was. Would Christians smoke and sleep with men from foreign countries? Would they have curse words in their daily language, and did they hang out at nightclubs and get drunk until 4 a.m.? Would Christians be in a relationship with someone of the same sex? Do they lie to their family or cheat on tests in school? Did they watch pornography or throw up their food? I asked myself the question, *Why in the world would they have me lead their church in worship on Sunday morning?* I guess this was what they meant when they asked me to pray about it. But my greatest question was, *How does God feel about all of this? Am I even welcome here?*

Little did I know this was the table God began to prepare for me the day I cried out for help. It was the day my girlfriend proposed to me and it was the day I realized my life had to change.

I've always admired the life of a Christian, a true authentic Christian who doesn't just talk the talk but also walks it out. I can tell if a person understands who they really are based on whether there is constancy and contentment. That's true for both Christian and non-Christian. But for authentic Christians, I see something deeper. I sense an inner strength that leans on a peace when life around them turns to chaos and a profound understanding when they lose something or someone they love. There is a well of joy they draw from when despair overtakes their heart, and an unswerving faith when they swim upstream against the current of our society.

But what strikes me the most is that authentic Christians are very aware they are truly known by the God of the Universe, the God who gave them the breath of life, and the God who to the majority of the world is unreachable. Beyond being truly known by God, they know without a doubt that God loves them.

But you, O LORD, know me; you see me, and test my heart toward you. (Jeremiah 12:3)

This is the love that I have always searched for. To know that I am not alone in this big scary world, that I am safe and that someone is looking out for my best interest. But for years I questioned if I was worthy enough to have it. I knew deep down that something was "off" in my life but I didn't know how to change my ways. All I had were questions and no answers.

But the longer I lingered in the world, independent from God, the deeper I grew in my own personal religion, the "my way or the highway" religion. I am sure you are familiar with it. It's the religion that shies away from any type of theology or accountability. It's created out of survival. If I am going to survive this life, the only thing I can trust is myself and what I believe to be true—not what some book dictates to me. But when I chose independence from God, I gave my life up for the taking. For years I chose to create my own instructions for life, but they were all based on my fears, failures, and insecurities. My identity became the very thing I was afraid of and life got blurry. I thought I was in control of my life but the truth is, I was under another set of orders. I put my life in the hands of this unstable world and allowed other people—who also were lost and lacking an identity—to guide me. Life was unsafe, filled with chaos, lies, and pain. It took me fifteen years to realize that I was empty, controlled, and lost, not to mention completely mixed up in my beliefs and my idea of love.

We don't yet see things clearly. We're squinting in a fog, peering through a mist. But it won't be long before the weather clears and the sun shines bright! We'll see it all then, see it all as clearly as God sees us, knowing him directly just as he knows us!

(1 Corinthians 13:12, MSG)

CHAPTER 9

Swing Wide

My answer was yes. I told the choir director that I "prayed" about it and yes, I would sing the song the following Sunday. I wasn't sure if the rest of the choir would be happy about this since I'd only been with them for less than a month. I had a little over a week to prepare a song. When I popped the CD in my car to give it a first listen I started to panic a little. Not only was it a gospel song but it was also a good seven minutes in length! The woman singing it had a power and flexibility to her voice that I could never match. The whole week I listened to this beautiful Brooklyn Tabernacle song called "I Never Lost My Praise" day and night, night and day. There was so much going on in the song that I needed to break it down to hear the bones of it—verse 1, chorus, verse 2, bridge, chorus—it all seemed like a blur to me because of all the extra ad-libs throughout the song.

I kept trying to copy exactly what she did but it was a disaster! If you've ever been to karaoke then you'll know what I'm talking about when I say I sounded like an opera singer trying to rap, or a heavy metal singer trying to yodel.

Wednesday finally rolled around and we had choir rehearsal. I was extremely nervous to sing in front of my peers because they'd never heard me before. I think I was more nervous about being judged for how badly I would sing the song.

My history with singing falls into the perfection category. When I was a little girl my parents introduced me to all sorts of musical styles, and the one that caught my attention was opera. I love everything about it. I love how strong the singers and vocals are and how loud they are able to sing. The first Broadway show I ever saw was *The Phantom of the Opera*, and I was mesmerized by the experience. I even had a favorite restaurant because it was named after the famous opera singer Luciano Pavarotti. Opera music was powerful and exquisite at the same time. I even asked my mom if I could take harp lessons. I thought if I could sing opera and play a sophisticated instrument like the harp that I would be ahead of my competition! So she rented a big harp, and I attempted to learn. I loved the sound so much I would push my ear up against the vibration and eventually got an earache. And that was the end of my harp career. Eventually, my love for opera turned into a love for musical theater in general. I would sing along to the soundtracks and try to match my voice entirely. I wanted to sing just like them.

As I got older and started exploring other styles of music I carried my perfectionism with me. I sang at many different venues over the years and was always given songs to sing. So I would learn them the best way that I could. If I couldn't hit a note or perform the same ad libs, I would just rearrange the parts so that I could mask it. So as I was learning this new song for the church, I was overwhelmed with panic because there were so many ad-libs in the song and I didn't know how to mask it.

I made it through rehearsal, and I was super encouraged by the choir. But I left church that night feeling like something was off. It was the beginning of October, so it was a chilly, rainy evening, and as I drove home from rehearsal I kept singing the song over and over again. I began to get frustrated because I couldn't hit the same notes she was hitting. I knew I had the potential to do it but I felt like something was blocking my throat; something was gripping my vocal cords. I finally pulled up to my apartment and sat in the car for a while. I kept asking myself, *Keri, what are you doing? How in the world are you going to sing the song at church on Sunday in front of thousands of people? What if you blank out? What if your voice cracks? What if you make a fool of yourself attempting to sing a gospel song?* I started to feel like I didn't belong. And I feared the church would see right through me. They would see who I really was, a girl trying to pass as a perfect Christian. I finally stopped singing along and just listened to the singer's voice. Numb from crying for the last hour, I sat in defeat and started to hear something different in her. What was it about her voice? There was something flawless about her imperfections that felt so wonderful to listen to. She had a strong voice but soothing at the same time. This woman apparently had something that I didn't have. In that very moment, I started to cry out, "I can't do this... I can't do this... I can't do this on my own." Then out of the blue I cried out, "I can't do this without You."

I've had a lot of moments in time but none of them have ever felt as real as this one. No sooner had I spoken those words than Jesus revealed Himself to me. My body went numb and my arms grew heavy. My heart sensed an old familiar flicker of joy and my spirit recognized a holy presence. The air went silent and the rain stopped. I felt my tingling hands slowly open and I felt an angelic-like bond form around my body.

And there He was, my best friend, the true love of my life... my Jesus.

I was frozen still in my car and couldn't move a muscle. But I didn't want to move. This was the moment I had been praying for since I was sixteen years old—the treasure I had been searching for all those years. With every turn of my life, from relationships to different religions and ways of life, it was always my ultimate goal to find Jesus again. I sat in my car for a good forty-five minutes and just talked to Him. I was so moved by His presence that I kept crying. I was heart to heart with Jesus but still had my heavy, overpacked bags of shame with me. Jesus lifted my head and said, "You don't have to carry these anymore." Instantly, I felt an unexplainable love and gave it all to Him. The weight of every shameful and guilty act I've ever committed fell off my shoulders and I knew I was safe with Him. This night changed me and I knew my whole world was about to shift.

I continued to have conversations with Jesus throughout my days and sharing about how nervous I was for the upcoming Sunday service at church. In my prayer time He gave me wisdom on what worship truly was. He described the responsibility that I had as I was about to lead the congregation. And He said He would be with me, and all I had to do was open my mouth, let go of myself, and sing. Sunday morning rolled around and I continued to stay in prayer. Five minutes before the 9 a.m. service started, I walked to the back of the stage and found a small little corner. I told Jesus,

"Don't forget You said You would meet me up there at the front of the stage. Remember, I said I couldn't do this without You." He assured me in my heart that He would.

They handed me a microphone and I stepped out to the front of the stage. I was brand-new to the church so nobody really knew who I was. I am certain they saw my legs shaking and my lips quivering but I closed my eyes anyway, thanked Jesus for being with me, and opened my mouth. I'm pretty sure I blacked out for the whole seven minutes of the song because I don't remember much. What I do remember was the response after. People did give me accolades for my voice but what I heard the most was that they experienced a shift not only in their hearts but in the church that morning. They kept using the word "anointed." I didn't know what it meant so I asked my friend at choir. She said it's the Holy Spirit flowing through you. It's when God's heart touches someone else's heart through your heart. She shared how God anoints people who love Him more than they love themselves.

Once she explained what anointing meant, I remembered my moment in the car when I was listening to the woman singing the gospel song. I recognized that she had something different in her. I couldn't put my finger on it, but whatever it was I felt myself being drawn to God. I heard the anointing on the gospel singer and I knew that Sunday morning God had anointed me to do the same thing. And for that I was grateful.

Worship has become a powerful tool in my life, not only to help me enter a vulnerable place with God but also to help others do the same. I've learned that if I don't allow myself to expose my deepest feelings, regrets, pain, and dirty secrets to God—whether it's current or from the past—I risk closing myself off from what I most desire when I close my eyes at night: to know God has me. His eye is on me, wanting the best for me, loving me unconditionally. When I worship, I allow the deepest part of me to lock into the deepest part of God completely. This deep connection allows me to help others experience the same vulnerability.

I couldn't wait to get home that Sunday morning so that I could share all of this good news with my boyfriend, Grant. But he didn't want anything to do with it. This time, though, I didn't try to appease him. I finally had Jesus back in my life and I wasn't about to give Him up. Our relationship deteriorated over the next few days and Grant ended up canceling his flight the following week. We broke up and I was beyond devastated. It put me into a very deep depression and I became obsessed with trying to get him back. But within the obsession I knew Jesus was tugging on the other end of the rope. It became a tug of war. It was hard for me to let Grant go because he was the love that distracted me from my homosexual life. He showed me what it looked like to be loved by a man and I didn't want to lose that. Deep down I knew that I had to, but I didn't know what God had in store for me. So the battle for my soul forged ahead. I would spend hours trying to connect with Grant, five thousand miles away, and then when it didn't work out Jesus was there to comfort me in the night. Looking back, I believe God allowed for Grant to be just a distraction and also a seed of hope to allow me to experience what it was like to be loved by a man. Of course, at the time I didn't know this so I fought hard to keep him. But every time

Grant asked me to put my faith aside, I couldn't do it. At the end of the day, Jesus won my heart over and over again.

It was a good thing I had my sweet dog with me. Hope and I rescued her when we lived in California and Cookie had been living with her until her new girlfriend couldn't take our dog in. I decided to find an apartment that would allow a pit bull, and Cookie officially became mine. She was my angel and I believe she had a sense of gratitude that we rescued her from the streets of LA. However, my life had to shift because I now had a dog that was battling cancer. It felt nice to care for something other than myself. It was me, Cookie, and Jesus every night struggling through my loss of Grant. Whenever sadness came over me, I did what my choir friends encouraged me to do: read the Bible.

I am so grateful for those years at my home church. I had a sense of belonging and a place to call my spiritual home. It's where I grew my faith and learned how to dive into the richness of God's Word. Scriptures were the only thing that could save me when I felt like I was spiraling out of emotional control. God met me in words and filled me with wisdom to help me fight the pull from the world. It wasn't easy to let go, not only of Grant, but also of the way I used to think and what I based my truth on. Not only did Grant abandon me for my faith, but so did a few of my friends from my past. Many people had the opinion that I was losing myself in my faith. I felt like I was kicking and screaming as I tried to let go of the world and what it brought into my life.

My heart would break over the things I didn't understand, but knew I had to let go. Yet God was so gentle and patient with me, which made me want to be close to Him. I knew I was safe with the Lord and that He would never leave my side, so it was vital for me to cultivate my relationship with Him.

I finally started to love music again so I bought a keyboard. I didn't play very well even though I took piano lessons when I was younger. But I still fiddled around on the keys at night when I felt sad. I had a melody that I couldn't stop playing. I would play the same thing over and over again, just a few melodic chords, until the wee hours of the night. Sometimes I would almost hear a melody echo back to me. I thought maybe I was losing my mind but I assumed it was something coming from my own creative mind. I hit an emotional wall one night, and the darkness was creeping in. The Lord brought to my mind a song I once heard about how the deep called out to deep. My curiosity shifted my attention to the Internet to see what this actually meant. This search led me to the book of Psalms.

> As a deer pants for flowing streams, so pants my soul for you, O God. My soul thirsts for God, for the living God. When shall I come and appear before God? My tears have been my food day and night, while they say to me all the day long, "Where is your God?" These things I remember, as I pour out my soul.
>
> (Psalm 42:1–4)

I didn't know who David was but, wow, was he speaking my language! I couldn't wait to read more so I kept going...

> Why are you cast down, O my soul, and why are you in turmoil within me? Hope in God; for I shall again praise him, my salvation. (Psalm 42:5)

Yes, "Why are you so sad, Keri?" I said to myself. And, "Oh yeah, I forgot I am supposed to put my hope in God." It was nice to know I wasn't the only one feeling disturbed inside. I went back for more...

Deep calls to deep at the roar of your waterfalls; all your breakers and your waves have gone over me. (Psalm 42:7)

There it was, the phrase "deep calls out to deep"! I was so excited to find it in the Bible! Then I wondered, what does it mean? So I kept reading...

By day the LORD commands his steadfast love, and at night his song is with me, a prayer to the God of my life. (Psalm 42:8)

That is where the Lord met me that night. It no longer was about my soul being downcast or being disturbed within. I still wanted to know what the phrase "deep calls out to deep" meant, but what caught my attention was "at night his song is with me." The Lord met me every single night at my cheap little keyboard, and as I played a little childish melody to Him, He was singing a song back to me. He was with me and that brought me so much comfort. It was more comfort than what Grant could offer me, more comfort than what the world could offer, and certainly more than what my friends could offer me. God was it. The ultimate comfort. The only one who could meet me in my place of desperation. And in understanding that, I finally learned what "deep calls out to deep" meant.

I wrote a song that night that I kept close to my heart for a very long time. Over the years I met with other writers and producers to help me tighten it up and put good music to it, but if I didn't like the direction it was going I put the process to a halt. I finally met with my good friends Chris and Anthony and they helped me to bring the song to life. It was born out of countless nights of depression and turned into the song I now get to share with others about my process of letting go of the world and finding peace in Jesus as a new believer.

Deep Calls to Deep
by Keri Cardinale, Anthony Hoisington, and
Chris Hoisington

Lord, you are here with me
In my daylight, in my dreams
You are here, by my side
Swaying me gently to heaven's lullaby

You're calling me, you're calling me over
You're calling me, you're calling me under

Your waves wash over me, your waves wash over me
Lord, how can it be … that you love me, you love me?
Lord, I go past the tides and the breakers
Into the arms of the maker
As deep calls out to deep
Your deep calls out to me

Lord, I know, I know that you're for me.
When I doubt, when I fear, I hear you, Father … Father

You're calling, calling, calling me
And I'll follow, follow where you lead

I was finally starting to come out of my hole of despair so I decided it was time to get involved in the ministry groups at church. I did them all—women's ministry, worship ministry, singles ministry, any type of outreach I could find! I was starting to see how God was positioning me in places that offered covering for me as I was navigating this new faith walk. My favorite place to be was in worship ministry. I loved everything about the choir, and I was starting to meet a lot of nice people. Every week the leaders picked different singers to be on the praise team, which was the wall of singers who stood at the front of the stage. The first time I was picked was the day I met Brett. He was extremely helpful and struck up a conversation with me. We started to talk about what we did for a living. I told him that at the time I was working for a doctor and he mentioned he was the manager of a local radio station. It happened to be the prominent Christian radio station in the Buffalo area but since I was new to the community I had never heard of it. I mentioned that I had interned at a country radio station during college down in Florida, which led him to ask me if I had a degree in communications. I do have a degree in communications but had never used it. A few weeks later I received an email from Brett asking if I would ever be interested in a career in broadcasting. This was the beginning of my life at WDCX radio. It was a significant shift for me, going from the medical field to broadcasting, but Brett took me under his wing and taught me all the tricks of the trade. He saw a potential in me and continued to train me up from a writer/producer, to program director, and eventually he was bold enough to put me on-air! He took a big chance on me and I'm so grateful he did.

Looking back, I am amazed at how fast God put me into the positions He created me for. It's as if God had everything lined up and ready to go as soon as I came home to Him. All of my assignments were ready, and He just guided me on where to go. Back in high school, when I had to make a decision on what to study in college, I originally wanted to be a social worker. But I thought it would be too hard to disconnect from my clients, so I chose Mass Communications, with a concentration in public relations. I was lucky enough to have the choice between Niagara University for theater or Florida Southern College for golf, because I got a partial scholarship for both. I am glad I decided on golf, even though I don't play anymore, because I would never have had the opportunity to work on radio if I didn't have my communications degree. Whether it's singing, speaking, or writing, God has called me to be a communicator. I never did anything with this calling because I never really had anything good to communicate. Because of Jesus, now I do.

I wasn't raised with preachers in suits and ties. I was raised with priests who wore clerical collars and vestments. But as a new believer I didn't care what you wore, I just wanted someone to teach me the truth. I was so hungry for it. I also wanted discipline in my life. I had lived so long without it, and it was exhausting trying to run my own life. I couldn't trust myself as the guide for my life and needed to put my trust in something higher than me. WDCX radio is a teaching-talk station that plays programs all day long filled with solid doctrine. I listened to it on my way to work, at work, and on my way home. Working at the station was one of the biggest blessings God has ever given me. It not only gave me the opportunity to grow deeper in my faith by what we provided the community, but the office was filled with incredible believers who would encourage each other on a daily basis. Of course, it was still an office, so we had our typical office drama at the water cooler, but it was a place where we chose to pray together every week. We celebrated wins and leaned on each other in the losses.

I had a lot of impurities that needed to be removed. I think God allowed the station to be an open atmosphere so that I had a safe place to allow these impurities to rise to the surface. I had many flaws in my old life that I unknowingly carried into my new life as a Christian. Slowly, one by one, they started to rise up. I was lucky enough to be surrounded by my brothers and sisters in Christ to walk me through it all.

My life was coming together and I was flying high in the Spirit! But the time was coming for me to understand the cost of what Jesus did for me on the cross. You see, all the shame He released me from had to go somewhere.

In May 2009, I was invited to a weekend getaway for my friend's birthday. She was a friend from my earlier years who happened to be a lesbian. I knew the weekend would be filled with lots of sex, alcohol, and possibly drugs. I was loving my life with Christ so I had no worries about going. As the weekend was getting closer, though, I started to feel hesitant. I reached out to my good friend from choir and asked for her opinion. She said it sounded like I was being convicted by the Lord. I had no idea what this meant so I asked her to explain. She went on to tell me that the Holy Spirit convicts us, or nudges us, to be wise in making decisions. The hesitation I was feeling was God trying to get my attention to make a wise decision about whether I should go away for the weekend. It's not that it would have hurt me, but I really had no business being in that scene anymore. It also meant I would have needed my ex-girlfriend to watch our dog so I would have had to make two trips to see her as well. The conviction was so firm that I had to say no. The birthday girl never spoke to me again after that but I felt really good about my decision. The only thing I was disappointed about was that I wouldn't be able to be in the choir that Sunday. They had a rule that if you missed rehearsal you couldn't be on the platform. But my parents decided to come to church with me that week so I was able to sit with them. What we were about to hear made me want to crawl out of my skin and slither my way out of the door.

Our pastor was in the middle of a series called "Elephants in the Church," and every week he talked about a topic that would normally be shied away from on a Sunday morning. One week was on evolution, another was about women in the church, and this Sunday was titled "The Rainbow Elephant." He was tackling the topic of same-sex attraction and how the church should respond. My mind was flooded with memories, one after the next. And as all these old files were coming out of my mental closet, I realized that my parents were sitting next to me. It's not that I forgot about the way I used to live; it was more that I didn't think it was worth discussing since I walked away from it. But that is not what God had in mind. Our pastor started breaking down Scripture from both the Old and New Testaments and describing the sinful nature of homosexuality. I'd never heard these things before. The only reason I knew it was sin was that the Catholic Church told me so. When I was living that life, I knew something was wrong but I could never put my finger on it. When my girlfriend and I broke our engagement after ten years together, I left the word "homosexuality" and all that it stood for in a box and hid it deep in my closet. I never wanted to talk about it again or even try to understand why it was part of me. All I knew was the shame attached to it and I was better off leaving it alone. As I read the Scriptures on the screen I secretly came undone inside, but I held it together until I was alone. I kissed my parents goodbye after we said it was a great service and we went our separate ways.

I got home and immediately opened the Bible again to reread everything I had learned that morning. I never knew how God felt about it, and that's when I realized why it caused me so much shame and regret.

The following Thursday I went to our church's singles ministry. The pastor was talking about making a list of sins. As I started to write them down, my old life flashed before my eyes. The list was a mile long and the more I wrote the more I realized what Jesus did for me. I called the pastor to show him this list and said, "I can't believe these are all the things I committed against God." Homosexuality was at the top of the list. We ended up having a great conversation and he asked if I would be willing to share my story with the group the following week. I was nervous to let this information out about my past, but I was more excited about how much Jesus loves me so I agreed to do it. The following week I gathered up enough courage to stand in front of the singles group and share my story. It was a bit choppy, to say the least, but it was my first time putting all the details into a testimony of God's incredible love and grace.

My story started traveling through the church and eventually made its way to a few of the leaders. Our pastor was preparing a message based on understanding the cost of Jesus' love and he was focusing on the sinful woman in Luke chapter 7 who washed the feet of Jesus. They were looking for a woman in our church who had a similar story. The sinful woman in the story came to believe in Christ's words deeply, embraced them, repented of her former way of life, and then did something concrete to demonstrate her repentance. She took action. They asked me if I would be willing to take action and share my story with the church. I agreed to do it, but then struggled with cold feet. I recorded my testimony video but I was overwhelmed with anxiety when I realized the entire church was going to find out about my past. It was okay for the small singles group to hear about it, but for the whole church and all the people who watch online...I almost pulled the plug. Were they just going to show that video? Was anybody going to vouch for me up there? What if they don't portray my story in the right way? I was so scared, I felt like I was coming out of the closet again. The week leading up to the service I found myself weeping. I would sit at my desk and random tears would roll down my face. At first I thought it was fear but then I realized that it was the beginning of my healing process. I was letting go of who I used to be. This allowed my story to come to light not only for me to see how God has transformed me but also to be a witness that it is possible to change.

I had no idea what his message was going to be about. I didn't even know it was about this specific Bible story. I was surprised to see just how similar my story was to the woman who washed the feet of Jesus with her tears. I went to church that day and sat in the back with a low baseball hat on my head. And as I listened to his message I saw my story come alive. And what once made me feel dirty and ashamed now made me feel so grateful for my relationship with Jesus. I realized that day my story is not about my past. Those are just details to help understand what I was saved from. My true testimony began the day I asked Jesus to take over my life.

My true testimony is all about Jesus, and giving God the glory that He deserves. He showered me with grace and mercy and gave me a second chance at life. He heard my cry in my desperate moment and responded by calling me home. He spoke loud enough to me so that I could hear Him.

The woman in the story had come to love Jesus and it was very genuine love. Her tears were not just tears of repentance for her sins; her tears were because she had come to love Jesus, and had never known what real love was before she met Christ. Jesus taught her to love. She may not have ever known her own human dignity and self-worth until she met Christ, who showed her that she was valuable in God's eyes and in His as well. This was my story as well, and it felt really good to share it.

Swing Wide
by Keri Cardinale, Anthony Hoisington,
Chris Hoisington, Justin Reynolds

Lord, You tell me that I can be known
I don't have to do this on my own
There are nights that I can't be sure
If Your love is all I'm looking for
'Cause I want to love You, the way You love me
And I want to know You, the way You know me

Swing wide, swing wide the doors of my heart
Swing wide, swing wide the doors of my heart
All my love, all my love for You

No sooner did the words come out of my mouth
You tore the veil and broke me down
You showed me in my weakness You are strong
You've been with me all along
'Cause I want to love You, the way You love me
And I want to know You, the way You know me

Swing wide, swing wide the doors of my heart
Swing wide, swing wide the doors of my heart
All my love, all my love for You

I've been holding on so long it seems
That what I hold has been holding me
I've been holding on so long it seems
That what I hold has been holding me
I've been holding on so long it seems
that You've been holding me

CHAPTER 10

A Lie versus the Truth

As I look back throughout my life, I can see how every step I took led me to the Lord. And two things helped me to do that:

1. I was self-aware and became open to the possibility that my "truth" could be wrong.
2. I decided to pay attention. I chose to acknowledge all the little signs and the way He was lighting my path, guiding me to Him and calling me home.

The reality is, my moment of true restoration began the day I cried out to God. The day Hope proposed to me I became self-aware and allowed myself to loosen up the ties of my own "truth" and consider the possibility of something far greater. Something holy. When I gave God attention in those three seconds of a heart cry, He heard me. I believe He heard me because my cry was a genuine request for a change. You see, a lot of times we say we want to change but are unwilling to let go of our view of truth. We are unwilling to give our lives enough space to see and hear the possibility of another truth.

Homosexuality was not my truth. But it was a version of a truth that I had clung to for a long time. The longer I hung on, the longer it became embedded in me and became my sexual identity.

Truth is like a stake in the ground. When you hammer it in, it goes so deep that it's very difficult to pull out. So in order to pull the stake out of the ground, you have to twist it back and forth and loosen it from the grip of the ground. You have to take your time. I believe the same goes for hearing the gospel. We all have our versions of how we choose to live our lives. And those versions get locked in. It's not easy to replace that with something new. It takes time for us to examine new ways of thinking to see if something is worth adding to our beliefs and way of life. God is patient and He will only give you as much information as you can chew and swallow at one time. The question is, are you willing even to hear what He has to say? I wasn't for many years. I wanted Him just to fix it and give me a good life. But His ways are better. His ways allow us to be involved. I came to that conclusion in my life because He revealed a new set of truths to me, and I responded by listening, contemplating, then applying them to see if it was a better way to live. To this day, I have yet to experience God's Word and not like how it affects my life. All of His reasons and principles are good because He is a good God.

We all have a desire to know God and to be known by Him. Some of us have more layers covering that up than others, perhaps from years of self-protection. We protect ourselves when we are hurt, angry, confused, and disappointed. These layers can turn into pride when we believe that we know what's best for our lives. We create our own natural order.

My desire, since I was a little girl, has always been to be close to God. To know Him and to love Him the way that He knows and loves me. I am the one who turned away from Him. But when—after years—I decided to hand over my "book of truth" and lay it down before God, that's when He took my hand and said, "Now I can show you how to live and you will be truly blessed."

Sinner. You are a big one, but I'm an even bigger sinner than you, so that should settle the score before I discuss sin. I know there are a thousand other detestable acts that we can pull out of the Bible, but I'm going to stick to the topic at hand. Please hear my heart and know that I'm not trying to dictate to you how you should live. I am sharing with you the things I have observed over the years. I am not here to challenge your beliefs or how you choose to live your life. One thing I have learned is to respect every person I meet. I want to offer myself as a no-judgment zone. I have come to have an appreciation for all walks of life and I love to hear people's stories! I am too busy examining my own life to be judging yours. But I do feel the responsibility to share what has impacted me the most.

So I am here to tell you that if you are struggling, or if there is a hint of a question in your heart about the way you are living, then I just ask that you give God a chance to show you another way.

This is how God changed me. And I'm grateful that He did. I believe the knowledge of sin is my biggest protection. It keeps me from having to deal with undesirable consequences and pain. I used to run from rules and preferred my independence over order.

But understand this, no one else could change me. Bits and pieces of Scripture were thrown in my face for years, but I couldn't understand what they meant. It was like hearing a foreign language. Truthfully, I don't think I was ready to accept God's truth. But once I opened up to it and accepted that God's Word was true I couldn't help but change. And the best part is, He gets all the glory for it. That's a win for me because I hate when people try to change me!

So here is the big question. Is homosexuality a sin? Yes, it is. It's a sexual sin, along with other sexual sins, like adultery and fornication. Stay with me.

Here are some verses about homosexuality that I found in the Old Testament:

You shall not lie with a male as with a woman; it is an abomination.
(Leviticus 18:22)

If a man lies with a male as with a woman, both of them have committed an abomination; they shall surely be put to death; their blood is upon them. (Leviticus 20:13)

I've been challenged that those verses are no longer applicable because they were under the law of the Old Testament. So here are a few passages that I found in the New Testament.

I have already shared this one in a previous chapter but for reference purposes I'm including it here as well.

For this reason God gave them up to dishonorable passions. For their women exchanged natural relations for those that are contrary to nature; and the men likewise gave up natural relations with women and were consumed with passion for one another, men committing shameless acts with men and receiving in themselves the due penalty for their error. And since they did not see fit to acknowledge God, God gave them up to a debased mind to do what ought not to be done. (Romans 1:26–28)

This next Scripture is lengthy but every word is important to read. It describes what happens when you ignore God and how it leads to a downward spiral.

For the wrath of God is revealed from heaven against all ungodliness and unrighteousness of men, who by their unrighteousness suppress the truth. For what can be known about God is plain to them, because God has shown it to them. For his invisible attributes, namely, his eternal power and divine nature, have been clearly perceived, ever since the creation of the world, in the things that have been made. So they are without excuse. For although they knew God, they did not honor him as God or give thanks to him, but they became futile in their thinking, and their foolish hearts were darkened. Claiming to be wise, they became fools, and exchanged the glory of the immortal God for images resembling mortal man and birds and animals and creeping things.

Therefore God gave them up in the lusts of their hearts to impurity, to the dishonoring of their bodies among themselves, because they exchanged the truth about God for a lie and worshiped and served the creature rather than the Creator, who is blessed forever! Amen. (Romans 1:18–25)

Sexual sin causes loneliness. Aside from the harm our rebellion does to our relationship with God, sin promises short-term pleasure and fulfillment but leaves you lonely and empty inside.

> *Flee from sexual immorality. Every other sin a person commits is outside the body, but the sexually immoral person sins against his own body. Or do you not know that your body is a temple of the Holy Spirit within you, whom you have from God? You are not your own, for you were bought with a price. So glorify God in your body.* (1 Corinthians 6:18–20)

I challenge you to read through the Scriptures with a fine-tooth comb. Allow God to reveal Himself to you. I don't believe for one minute that God is sitting on a cloud waiting to slap our hands with a ruler when we sin. I also don't think He sat on His throne at the beginning of time and had to decide what was sin and what wasn't. I believe God created His natural order in keeping with His character, and anything that falls outside of it or goes against it will naturally suffer the consequences. But I think the same goes for life in general, don't you think? Sexually speaking, would it be fair to say there are consequences for infidelity? If a husband cheats on his wife with his coworker, is that okay? Should it be no big deal? Everyone involved gets hurt, especially his wife. If you choose to sleep around with multiple partners and contract a sexually transmitted disease, would that be okay? Should it be no big deal? You love God, but if you did something to hurt your relationship with Him, would you be okay with God turning His back on you? Sin is any act of defiance or wrongdoing against divine order. Sin is also any thought or action that threatens to come between you and God.

His natural order is meant to protect us and our relationship with our Creator. God has written His Law on our hearts, and our conscience bears witness to this. God gives each of us an internal compass so we will know right from wrong.

> *They show that the work of the law is written on their hearts, while their conscience also bears witness, and their conflicting thoughts accuse or even excuse them.* (Romans 2:15)

I know what it feels like to have a wall up between God and me, and I don't ever want to experience it again.

> *Or do you not know that the unrighteous will not inherit the kingdom of God? Do not be deceived: neither the sexually immoral, nor idolaters, nor adulterers, nor men who practice homosexuality, nor thieves, nor the greedy, nor drunkards, nor revilers, nor swindlers will inherit the kingdom of God. And such were some of you. But you were washed, you were sanctified, you were justified in the name of the Lord Jesus Christ and by the Spirit of our God.* (1 Corinthians 6:9–11)

First Corinthians 6:9–11 has become my life verse. It reminds me that God didn't leave me behind. I was never too dirty for God to see me and clean me up. I have hope for a new day.

> *Hope does not put us to shame, because God's love has been poured into our hearts through the Holy Spirit who has been given to us.* (Romans 5:5)

CHAPTER 11

Wave the Freedom Flag

One afternoon in June 2015, I sat in my radio station office in Buffalo, New York, hosting our afternoon worship music show, when I received the news that same-sex marriage was legalized in the United States. It was blowing up my newsfeed on Instagram, Twitter, and Facebook. Both Christians and non-Christians I knew—family, church friends, and old friends alike—were changing their profile pictures in support of this Supreme Court decision. Rainbow flags were waving high in the air. As I watched the posts and comments, my eyes started to water, and for a brief moment, I felt alone.

I started to question God. *Was I wrong? Is this really something to be celebrated? Was all the work You did in my heart over the last eight years a big lie?* The world is celebrating "freedom." And I wondered if my freedom was a mistake.

God grabbed hold of my thoughts and my heart that day and said, *"Keri, your freedom was not a mistake."* Then as I opened my Bible to Psalm 40:1–5, the Lord spoke the words over my life.

"Keri, remember when you waited patiently for Me, and I turned to you and heard your cry? Remember when I lifted you out of the ditch, and pulled you from deep mud; when I stood you up on a solid rock and made sure you wouldn't slip. Remember when I put a new song in your mouth, a hymn of praise. More and more people are seeing this: they enter the mystery, abandoning themselves to me. Keri, blessed are you who give yourself over to Me. Turn your back on the world's 'sure thing'; ignore what the world worships. The world is a huge stockpile of God-wonders and God-thoughts. But nothing and no one comes close to this. What we have."

In that very moment, I don't think I've ever felt so close to Him. He reminded me of what He did in my life. He rescued me from the very thing the world was praising and celebrating. It was then that my freedom didn't seem so small anymore. The world was celebrating freedom . . . and so was I.

We all have freedoms in our lives worth celebrating. Some of us know what it feels like to be released from the grip of sin, and others are still waiting for the day it will happen. I have gained comfort in knowing that freedom comes in all shapes and sizes. It comes in all volume levels. As you are reading this, thoughts may be coming to your mind. Maybe you have experienced freedom from the guilt of having an abortion, or the freedom from fear or insecurity. Or like me, you have experienced freedom from sexual sin and a life of homosexuality. Maybe you've experienced freedom in everyday life situations. Sometimes we get caught up in measuring how big our testimonies are compared to other people. God knows the power of your freedom story and He reveals it to you privately, just you and Him alone, because He knows there will be a day when you will be challenged with wondering if you really are free from whatever you've been hanging on to. He knows there will be a day when you will have to be reminded of the sweetness of His power in your life. That is the true beauty of freedom. Freedom is celebrating your relationship with your Savior.

We all have the freedom to choose how we want to live. We even have the freedom to choose God. But we didn't have a choice about how, when, and where we were born. Scripture tells us that every human being was born with a bent toward sin. In fact, I believe I was bent toward many different sins, meaning I was born with the potential to rebel against God—just like we all were. It's in our DNA and goes all the way back to Adam and Eve. We all can develop specific sins and allow them to come into existence. Between our behavior patterns, our personal makeup, and what we have learned growing up, we have been provided with the conditions for sin that, in turn, entice us to act.

A coworker of mine was born with a high sex drive, and he's always tempted to sleep around and act on every lustful impulse— even with a married woman. Should I encourage him to embrace it or get help through counseling? He gets to make the choice. A friend of mine was born with a tendency toward drug use that's out of control. She almost lost her job. Should I encourage her to embrace it or get help to fight the addiction? She gets to make the choice.

Another friend has an addiction to money and greed and now has a gambling problem. He's on the verge of losing his house, and he has four kids. Should I encourage him to embrace it or get help to manage his money? He gets to make the choice. And my family member is genetically bent toward violence. He landed himself in jail and lost the right to see his daughter. Should I encourage him to embrace it or get help to manage his anger? He gets to make the choice.

Some say it's natural to feel the way I felt with same-sex attraction. It's also natural for me to be nasty, angry, impatient, and selfish. And it's natural for me to threaten people when I don't get my way. I would hope that someone would want me to get healthy instead of just embracing that I was born this way.

Sin is still sin, no matter how we spin it. But God has mercy for us and will always provide a way out.

> *No temptation has overtaken you that is not common to man. God is faithful, and he will not let you be tempted beyond your ability, but with the temptation he will also provide the way of escape, that you may be able to endure it.* (1 Corinthians 10:13)

I think we tend to miss this next part, and for the majority of us, Christian and non-Christian, we have a hard time grasping the big picture. God sent Jesus to die on the cross to pay the price for our rebellion against God.

I'm no preacher so I will let the Scripture speak for itself.

> *This is the kind of life you've been invited into, the kind of life Christ lived. He suffered everything that came his way so you would know that it could be done, and also know how to do it, step-by-step.*

> *He never did one thing wrong,*

Not once said anything amiss.

They called him every name in the book, and he said nothing back. He suffered in silence, content to let God set things right. He used his servant body to carry our sins to the Cross so we could be rid of sin, free to live the right way. His wounds became your healing. You were lost sheep with no idea who you were or where you were going. Now you're named and kept for good by the Shepherd of your souls. (1 Peter 2:24,25, MSG)

It took me a long time to realize, when Jesus met me in my car that October day, His love was so strong that my bent toward sin turned a different direction. When I opened my heart to God, He rushed right in because He was standing outside the door all along. The moment He entered my heart was the moment my sin was face to face with His holiness. Sin was crushing me, but God crushed my sin. This is why I could never do it on my own. It was too much for me to bear. God freed me from my sin, and I could finally breathe.

So as much as the world is allowed to wave their flag and celebrate freedom, I too am allowed to wave my flag of freedom, even if I'm alone in my own little corner.

A word from my heart: I am not here to judge or criticize you if you are in a homosexual relationship. I have many friends who are, and I love them for who they are and the joy they bring into my life. It is your choice, not mine. I hope you won't judge or criticize me for my choices. The words that I write are based on my personal experience, my interpretation of what the Lord has shown me over the years, and my observations. I pray that you at least give God a chance to show you His version of the life He created you for.

CHAPTER 12

Love Restored

Some people say it's impossible to change, but I know it is possible. There is a word I would like to use that might not make sense to some. The word is "sanctification." Let me explain. The more I came to understand God and how His kingdom operates, my mind allowed me to apply some of the spiritual principles that I learned. Over time, I realized God changed me without me even knowing it. My relationship with my mom changed; we are now closer than ever. And the same goes for my dad. I was able to let the junk between my sister and I go, and because of that we are real friends, not just family. I have learned to allow my brother to find his way, just like I had to find my own way, and support him with love as he finds his way through life.

My sexual desires changed as well. But it wasn't because I decided not to be a lesbian anymore. I decided to learn who I really was and to understand my true identity. My sexuality naturally fell back in order . . . God's divine order. I've come to learn that it was the labels I applied to myself that kept me in a place of confusion for so long. Just because I kissed a girl didn't mean I was gay. I know it's important for us to understand who we are and what we stand for. It gives us purpose. But we don't leave much room when we start slapping labels on ourselves. I've talked to so many people who realized years later that they were never the person they claimed to be. I found out later in life that I wasn't 100 percent in agreement with my self-titled sexual identity.

My parents were the very first people to believe in me. They gave me, my sister, and my brother everything we needed to survive and succeed in this life here on earth. I struggled with my relationship with my family for a long time. We could never connect because I was always trying to be a different version of me. I figured I had nothing else to live for so I might as well create a persona that stood out and gave me something to believe in and fight for. For a while, I was trying to figure myself out and force myself to believe I was a homosexual. My family knew the real me.

As my life started to shift toward a new truth and a new way of life, my relationship with my family naturally fell into place. As much as everyone has a responsibility for what they bring to the table, the things I brought were filled with chaos, bitterness, and lies. When I removed all of those things and started to fill my life with the characteristics of Jesus, our relationship bloomed. To this day we still have yet to discuss my past and all of my wild adventures through life. But I know they see a change in me. Even at my age it still feels nice to have proud parents, and I cherish my relationship with them.

I could never tell if my mom knew my life was changing until one day she told me her friend came to her for advice about her own daughter. My mom told her the daughter should connect with me because she saw the light in me. She basically told me the story and put me in the third person. I got off the phone that day and thanked God for restoring my mom's faith in me. My dad, on the other hand, likes to tell me and everyone else that I am a minister of the Word! I always laugh but deep down it is so beautiful to know that my father sees holiness in me.

I never really restored relationships with my ex-girlfriends from the past even though it would have been nice since they were my very close friends. But, unfortunately, I have set boundaries for their sake and for mine. I see them on social media from time to time, and I see they are all doing well, and I celebrate their life accomplishments. But because we were so close, I am very aware of their deep wounds as well. I pray that they each find the same kind of love that restored me.

God fixed an area that has been a dysfunctional one for me for as long as I can remember. I had a distorted view of what a good female friendship looked like, and intimacy always played a role with any girl I was extremely close with. It allowed me to rely heavily on the female gender. They were my comfort, protection, and energy source when I was low. Over time I couldn't distinguish the difference between what I should have expected from a girl versus a boy. I allowed my friends to fulfill all the areas that were meant to be covered by a man. I trusted women but just a little too much. Friendships with women have a special place. This is no surprise since the first woman we were trained to rely on was our mother when we were in her womb. But just like many other areas of my personality, I tend to go to the extreme. As I struggled to find balance in my life, I would always swing from one side of the pendulum to the other, never landing in the middle. God restored this for me in so many ways. I have learned that my friends have a place in my life, but I had to set boundaries. One of my mottos is: "I'm not a pigtails-and-pillow-fights kind of girl anymore." Sometimes when a group of women get together, at any age from twelve even into their fifties, the gathering can have a slumber-party vibe. Girls do want to let their hair down; we do want to have fun, giggle, and be expressive. We like to talk about heartfelt topics, and we want someone to give us the time and space to get all of our thoughts out. Some men just don't have the capacity to sit and listen to a woman for three hours straight. But we can offer each other that freedom in a deep friendship.

God made us sexual beings, and I believe at any moment any of us (men or women) could have a split-second attraction to someone of the same sex. We all have a need for love and attention, but when it goes to the extreme and we let our moral walls down, we could find ourselves in a situation that we never had any intention of being a part of. I have heard many stories of two heterosexual women or men who allowed themselves to get so engrossed with each other as friends that it turned into a sexual act. Sex can turn into an addiction, just like any other act that fills a need. A recovering alcoholic knows what it feels like to be freed from the liquor chains. But they also know what the smell of their favorite drink is. So they set boundaries to keep them from ever going back, because they know what it cost to get free. Recovering food addicts have to make a wise decision when faced with an invitation to a family function. They know a food fest is in the near future, so they plan ahead for the temptation that's to come. Some may decide to skip the party while others follow their guidelines and stay on high alert. The family may not understand what the big deal is but the recovering food addict knows what it cost to fight the demons in their head. For me, my addiction to love and intimacy turned into an addiction to sexual relations with women. I know the what it cost to change, so I set up boundaries with friends because I never want to go back to that place again.

Some people don't understand it, but they aren't the ones fighting my battle. I am often asked if I am still attracted to women. My answer is no, and I can only give the credit to God for shifting my desires, but I am also aware that there is a real enemy who works twenty-four hours a day to create strategies to bring us down. I also know that, although the Lord allowed me to overcome this area in my life, in other areas I still need His help to have victory. We all have needs, but if we are not self-aware of what they are, we will find anything and anyone to fill it. God ultimately knows our needs better than we do ourselves. Spend time with Him to find the best way to fulfill them.

God has given me a new perspective on women in my life. I am grateful and couldn't live without them. Now that I know the purpose of a good friend, I can be confident in building healthy relationships. I have a circle of friends, both men and women, who have become my strength. They know my story, respect my boundaries, and encourage me to keep fighting for my faith. I pray that I offer them the same type of friendship.

In 2012, I received a surprise email from my first boyfriend. He asked how I was doing and gave me an update on his life and his daughters. He shared where he was living now and what he's doing for his career, and he wanted to know where we left off—if we hated each other or if we were civil. It took me a day or two to respond because I wasn't sure if I wanted to reconnect with him.

A friend of mine at work told me I had two options. I could either blow it off and say, "Hi, thanks for reaching out, have a great life." Or I could connect with him and see if God has some healing for both of us. And that's exactly what happened. We ended up talking on the phone for five hours and hashed out everything. There were things he told me that I never realized. I hurt him just as much as he hurt me. I never knew he was a virgin when we first had sex, so to find out we were in the same position allowed both of our defenses to come down. He is one of my best friends to this day, and I'm so grateful that God did work to restore what once was broken.

For years I worked endlessly when it came to my career. I went to college for communications but never used my degree. I also had a massage therapy license that was covered with dust. Within a few months of giving my life back to Jesus, I met my soon-to-be boss who offered me a career in radio. I was also able to start working part-time doing massage therapy, and God gave me the opportunity to sing again. I "made a deal" with Him and said I'd only sing for Him. No more bar karaoke for this girl!

There are a few areas of my life where I feel God is very clear with me on direction. The first is my ministry. He has shown me over the years that He is the one who will move mountains to make it happen. Every time I tried to go before Him prematurely, He would always gently set me back and encourage me to wait on Him. I use all the good things and talents He gave me for ministry, so naturally God should be the one to dictate when and where I will minister to people. The second area is my food addiction. He has been very loud and clear that He's not going to remove this like He did when He removed cigarettes from my life. This was an addiction that I had to come to an understanding of, so that I know what it costs to be healthy. He has provided every tool that I need to be healthy and fit. It comes down to me not being a couch potato. And the third area is my love life. The last time I gave my heart to someone was over ten years ago. I would cry myself to sleep sometimes wondering if I would ever have a relational love again here on earth. So for ten years I was single. But I can't even begin to tell you how much I cherish those years. It gave me time not only to grow close to the Lord but also to learn a lot about myself. I was self-sufficient, independent, and finally felt settled in my apartment in Buffalo. I came to the realization that it would be nice to have someone in my life, but I didn't need it. And then Philip James came along. It was January 2018 when I felt the urge to understand how to date. I had a brand new Keri Cardinale that has been restored, rewired, and renewed, and she wanted to experience going on a date!

It wasn't so much that I was lonely, but it was the companionship that I was hoping to find. I wanted to be the type of woman I learned about through God's Word over the last decade. I wanted to know what it felt like to really respect the man I was with and to experience all the love he had for me. I wanted to be beautiful for someone. So on January 6, 2018, I finally decided to make a list. I was always instructed to make a list of exactly what I wanted in a man. The last time I did that I ended up on DatingBritishguys.com, so this time I decided to list a few requests.

Dear God, I would love to have a male companion. A true lover. Where love is in his blood and bones. A man who loves me and understands who I am. Strong, attractive, secure, confident, protective, loving to others, compassionate, and kind. A man who is respected by others and complements my personality. And

God, I would love to have a man who can look past all of my shortcomings so that I never have to feel insecure with him.

I decided to get into the dating scene. My goal? To go on as many dates as I could! I just wanted to see what was out there and to know what it was like to sit across from a man. After a few doozies, I met Phil. His kind eyes caught my attention, and we went on our first date. For the first time in a long time, I felt like a woman. He had a strength about his personality that I was immediately attracted to. We had a pleasant conversation and agreed that it would be nice to go out on a second date. And yes, he paid! Over the next few months, Thursday became our date night. And I enjoyed every single one without the pressure of feeling like I needed more. He knew I hadn't dated in a long time and I found myself attracted to how secure he was in himself and our dating pattern. After watching him interact with my family, his own family, and my friends, I realized that I was falling in love with him. The moment I felt it, I went back to the list I made in my notebook. He had everything I asked for. And I began to cry when I started to realize what was happening.

Phil is a man who waited patiently to find true love. He lives a steady life and prefers the simple things. For me, I was never patient and ended up going in all sorts of directions on the hunt for love. My life was never steady, and I thrived on chaos over simplicity. That was all until Jesus intervened and saved my life. Being with Phil has become a part of my testimony because I am able to celebrate now who I have grown into as a woman. I can embrace my femininity and never apologize for it. I don't have to demand respect because he showers me with love and affection, and in return, I adore him for the man he is, and I love to encourage him and all that he does. Early in 2019, Phil and I exchanged our wedding vows, and I am so proud to call him my husband.

Some days I stop what I am doing and take a good look at my life. And when I compare it to God's Word, I am blown away. This is the amazing God I have chosen to serve, and it's the God I feel so blessed by every day my life. I'm so grateful that He heard my cry and gave me a brand-new life. This Scripture explains it best:

> God, your God, will restore everything you lost; he'll have compassion on you; he'll come back and pick up the pieces from all the places where you were scattered. No matter how far away you end up, God, your God, will get you out of there ... God, your God, will outdo himself in making things go well for you: you'll have babies, get calves, grow crops, and enjoy an all-around good life. Yes, God will start enjoying you again, making things go well for you just as he enjoyed doing it for your ancestors. But only if you listen obediently to God, your God, and keep the commandments and regulations written in this Book of Revelation. Nothing halfhearted here; you must return to God, your God, totally, heart and soul, holding nothing back. This commandment that I'm commanding you today isn't too much for you, it's not out of your reach. It's not on a high mountain—you don't have to get mountaineers to climb the peak and bring it down to your level and explain it before you can live it. And it's not across the ocean— you don't have to send sailors out to get it, bring it back, and then explain it before you can live it. No. The word is right here and now—as near as the tongue in your mouth, as near as the heart in your chest. Just do it! (Deuteronomy 30:3,4,9–13, MSG)

The blessings are in abundance when you walk with the Lord, when you hand Him the keys to your life and say, "Take it and do what You want with it." It's time to turn in your keys and let the Master fix what's been broken and make all things new. Give God a chance to show you just how much He loves you.

CHAPTER 13

The Heart of Ministry

"It's my mission field."

"She is my project."

"He's been coming to church for a while, but at some point, someone needs to tell him the truth."

"She doesn't love Jesus because she's gay."

"That's the gay couple sitting over there. Clearly they refuse to turn from their sin; otherwise, they wouldn't still be together."

These are just a few of the comments I have heard about how Christians "minister" to the homosexual community. The people they are talking about had names and are made in the image of God. Somehow, we've put the sin on a pedestal and left the person standing with no dignity left.

I became a Certified Life Coach so that I could expand my ministry. I see clients from many ends of the spectrum—from teens trying to figure out what "label" they fall under to homosexuals who feel rejected by loved ones. I have clients who are confused about how they feel and don't want to experience same-sex attraction. But I also get parents who, like mine, just want their son or daughter back. This specific sexual sin causes so much confusion, frustration, and anger. It not only causes splits in relationships but can eventually create a fit of rage toward God.

If you know someone who is living a homosexual lifestyle, you may be struggling with what to do, what to say, how to say it, and what to believe. But deep down the truth is that you want this person to change. We can't change anyone, but we can influence. I only hope that I can help someone based on all the wisdom God has given to me. Being a follower of Christ is an honor. We need to humble ourselves. What if, instead of putting the sin on the pedestal, we put God there instead?

I want you to think about the person in your life who is gay. What do you know about them? What are their goals, personality quirks, and fears? What makes them laugh, what were their parents like, and how was their childhood? Did they get bullied? Abused? Do they feel alone? Insecure? Lost, or unstable? Scared? How do they really view themselves as just who they are without a label?

Could you be their friend regardless of their sexual orientation? Does your son or daughter have a place at the dinner table?

The answers are simple. Either they are in your life, or they are not. I have come to realize I don't believe in short-term mission with people in my life. If that person is special to me, then I want to make it for the long haul.

As Christians, we often enter into the person's life with a motive to change them, or to share biblical truth, but I'll bet they already know the truth of God's Word just like I did. They may already have a trust issue, maybe even with God. Most likely they will have a trust issue with you as well.

Have you ever thought to ask this person if they had any interest in knowing God?

Sometimes just asking a person what they think about God is a start to a great conversation.

There is something I would like to plant in your mind, and that's never to give up hope on the people you love and care for. Operating in God's timing is difficult, but it's crucial. If you know someone who is living a homosexual lifestyle, just know that person has the same deep desires that you do: a more profound sense of love and acceptance. I've come to learn that God wired us with this desire. We get distracted by the counterfeit love out there, but we eventually find our way back home.

We all have a choice on how to respond to God, and it was God who gave us that freedom. I made a decision to shut down my relationships in the world and hold still. That's when God knew I was ready to hear Him. I had to pay attention to what was happening in my spirit to admit to myself that I wanted something more.

This is true ministry, to homosexuals or to anyone: loving people right where they are and always sharing the gospel. Just remember the gospel isn't about sexual preferences; it's about Jesus Christ. Change starts with Him.

I want to encourage you to ask God to give you a new perspective on how to love the person who chooses homosexuality. Ask God to provide you with fresh opportunities to show them Jesus' character, and for God to increase your patience. Understand that all you can do is love, share the truth in love, and trust the Holy Spirit to move. It's amazing how sometimes it becomes a test of our own faith. We are all works in progress. Sometimes God uses difficult times to reveal areas in our lives that need some attention.

True conversion to the Lord, I believe, happens best when you are alone with Him. God was patient with me and met me in my quiet place. He created the most beautiful space for us to reconnect and because it was so intimate, I will never forget it. It has become the story of my life.

AFTERWORD

The realities I faced, the loneliness I experienced, and the heartache of broken relationships are what gave me the strength to carry on my journey. I don't regret one ounce of it. In fact, if I could have a banquet, I would invite my family, friends, church community, the gay community, every person I met, slept with, fought with, and prayed to different spirits with, and we would have a feast! It would be more than just a celebration of where I finally landed in life; it would be an appreciation banquet—a thank-you for all the marks and impressions that have been left on my heart, all the pain that propelled me forward on my quest for a better life. And I would place an apology card on everyone's plate, to say I'm sorry for dragging you through my mud. My prayer is that you can forgive me and trust me when I tell you the journey to God is worth it. Because we are all on a journey to fill the void in our hearts. I just know now that it's only Jesus who can fill that void. God created each of us with a void, a longing for Him. He is the compass, and He will always lead us home.

BEAUTY FROM ASHES
Donna Sparks

In a transparent and powerful manner, the author reveals how the Lord took her from the ashes of a life devastated by failed relationships and destructive behavior to bring her into a beautiful and powerful relationship with Him. The author encourages others to allow the Lord to do the same for them.

Donna Sparks is an Assemblies of God evangelist who travels widely to speak at women's conferences and retreats. She lives in Tennessee.

www.story-of-grace.com

www.facebook.com/
donnasparksministries/

www.facebook.com/
AuthorDonnaSparks/

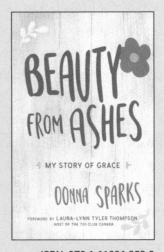

ISBN: 978-1-61036-252-8

To my parents, Joe and Diane Cardinale,
for knowing who I was when I didn't know myself